100 Duet Scenes

FOR Teens

One-minute duos for student actors

Michael Moore

MERIWETHER PUBLISHING LTD.
Colorado Springs, Colorado

Meriwether Publishing Ltd., Publisher
PO Box 7710
Colorado Springs, CO 80933-7710

www.meriwether.com

Editor: Theodore O. Zapel
Assistant editor: Amy Hammelev
Cover design: Jan Melvin

Library of Congress Cataloging-in-Publication Data

Moore, Michael, 1954 Dec. 24-
  100 duet scenes for teens : one-minute duos for student actors / by Michael Moore. -- 1st ed.
      p. cm.
  ISBN 978-1-56608-187-0
1. Young adult drama, American. I. Title. II. Title: One hundred duet scenes for teens.
  PS3613.O5655A614 2012
  812'.6--dc23

                                    2012003274

1   2   3   12   13   14

Dedicated

To

My Lovely Wife,

Helen

Table of Contents

Preface

As a theatre teacher for twenty years, I've often been faced with the problem of providing my students with acting material that was both challenging and beneficial, but that could be mastered in just a day or two. I also found that the scenes provided in many theatre classroom textbooks were inadequate to meet my students' needs. The scenes provided in these texts were certainly from worthy plays, but without a previous knowledge of the plays, my students were left at a disadvantage in both understanding and interpreting the scenes.

My purpose in writing this collection of one-minute plays is to address this problem. These scenes were written to assist classroom theatre teachers in developing their students' acting skills. Each scene is complete in that it has a definite beginning, middle, and end. Each one highlights or explores a particular personality trait, or emotion, or situation. Some of the scenes are highly dramatic, but most are comic since that seems to appeal the most to young performers. A few are just plain off the wall. Regardless, this variety should provide young actors ample opportunities to exhibit and develop their acting skills.

Also, because the scenes are brief, the students can handily memorize the scenes in a short amount of time. So much of the work in acting is simply memorization. The quicker and easier an actor can accomplish this task, the sooner he or she can start bringing a character to life. These scenes provide performers with a plethora of opportunities to develop their memorization "muscles" and give them interesting and challenging pieces to perform as well. It's my hope that after mastering some of these short scenes, students will feel better prepared for moving on and tackling the larger roles that await them!

— Michael Moore
November 2011

1

Acknowledgments

Special thanks go to my daughter, Mary-Nancy Smith, for proofreading this manuscript and her many good suggestions.

Thanks to everyone at Meriwether Publishing for their belief in this project, especially Amy Hammelev for all her editing work.

Also, thanks to God for his grace and mercy on a daily basis.

Notes about Performing the Scenes

Introducing a Scene

Since the scenes are short, an introduction is appropriate to clue in your audience as to the *who, where, when,* and *why* of the scene they are about to watch. The introduction for each scene has been written to assist in communicating this information. It can be read aloud prior to performance in order to set up the performance. In most of these, the two characters are named (always capitalized) and further information is given to set up the locale and the immediate situation. For other scenes, the introduction offers none of this information, but hopefully provides enough information to arouse the reader's and the audience's curiosity. These introductions can be delivered by the actors performing the scene, or by the classroom teacher, or by a third student. Also, actors should feel free to create their own introductions.

Stage Directions

These are given throughout most of the scenes to denote actions that actors need to undertake while performing the scenes. In other words, items framed by parentheses ( ) and written in italics are never meant to be spoken.

For example: *(BO and JO are standing at the end of a pier and are fishing.)*

Italics

These are used two different ways in the scripts. First, all stage directions and all vocal directions are written in italics and framed with parentheses.

Second, in dialogue, a specific word may be written in italics to show that it conveys a meaning that is not directly apparent in the regular use of the word and that the word is supposed to be delivered with extra vocal emphasis.

For example: "What do you mean you bought *another* car?"

What the character is really trying to say is, "Another car? But we just bought a new car last week!"

Vocal Directions

These are given to assist the actor in identifying words in the dialogue that need to be given extra stress when spoken. Most often, these are written immediately after the speaker's name is listed. Sometimes, they may be inserted into the middle of a character's speech, but either way, they are always written in italic and framed by parentheses.

For example: BOB: *(Screaming)* Where have you been? *(Quieter)* No. No. I'm not going to talk to you like that.

A Beat

Often in the scenes you will see this: *(A beat).* These are all written in italics and framed by parentheses. They represent a moment of silence. What "a beat" does not represent is a moment of inactivity! What it does signify is that something is going on inside the character's head! He or she may be thinking of what to say next or perhaps a new idea has popped into his or her head. Either way, the struggle to come up with what to say next will almost always display itself facially or bodily. Good actors work to show that these transitions are happening inside the character.

Punctuation

The written English language is an imaginative and wonderful collection of symbols — letters for words and punctuation marks — that help us communicate to each other. This is why we all take English class! In particular, punctuation symbols help writers organize their words so they make sense and convey the meaning they intended. These are all invaluable little devices for actors in saying their lines effectively, and they aid more closely in interpreting what the playwright had originally imagined in his or her head.

A quick review of these may be helpful because they do play such big roles in an actor's interpretation and delivery of dialogue.

Periods (.) — These tell the speaker that they have reached the end of a sentence, the end of a thought, and that this is a good place to pause and take a breath.

Commas (,) — These are used to separate words in lists, proper names of people, adverb clauses, and prepositional phrases at the beginning of sentences. They help us give certain words or phrases their own due.

Colons (:) — Ordinarily, these mean what follows after it is very important — pay attention to it. For example: "There's something I think you need to know: Joanie is not your friend!"

Semi-colons (;) — These usually separate two complete thoughts that are not joined by a conjunction. For example: "He fell asleep in class; it was first period."

Exclamation marks (!) — Usually this is a short expression delivered with much emotion and generally these are very emphatic. For example: "I just got engaged!"

Question Marks (?) — The speaker is asking for information or clarification. We all know what these are, right?

Combination Exclamation and Question Marks (!?) — These are sometimes used on questions that also are meant to express surprise, shock, or disbelief by the speaker. For example: "You threw the cat out of the window?!"

Ellipses (...) — This signifies that the voice trails off — usually with a downward inflection on the last word prior to the ellipses. Generally, this means the character is lost in thought and pauses for a moment as he or she tries to find the right word to say next or to organize his or her thoughts further. For example: "I don't know how to ... Gee, I hate this ... Lisa, I'm leaving you."

Dashes (—) — These can stand for one of the following. First, they can represent quick, abrupt interruptions in a character's speaking. This generally means the character is stammering or stuttering as he or she attempts to say the right word. The character is not pausing to gather his or her words or thoughts, but is rushing ahead. For example: "I — uh — I — Look, can we talk about this later?"

Second, dashes can be used to signify that the initial sentence is being interrupted and new information is being interjected prior to continuing with the sentence. For example: "We saw these kids — Aerik and Kali, I think — walking with this really, really, big dog."

5

Contractions (') — We use these all the time in conversation. We shorten verbs and attach the remainder to a noun or pronoun using an apostrophe. They're just funny to see in print. Examples: Bob's going to the store. We're going with him. It's our turn!

Changing Character Names

The character names used in most of the scenes have purposely been selected to be very generic. As long as you and your teacher agree, it is OK to change them for your performance.

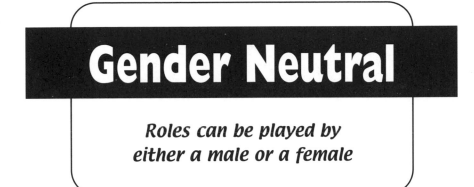

Gender Neutral

*Roles can be played by
either a male or a female*

Appreciative

Introduction
Sometimes, it's good to stop and smell the roses. In this scene, two gnomes, PAT and JO, discuss their career situation. They wear pointy hats and carry backpacks.

1 PAT: Here's the latest shipment of dusty bunnies to put
2   under the bed, Jo. You been out collecting?
3 JO: Yeah, what else do I ever do, Pat? There was a truckload
4   of stuff in the carpet today. Nail clippings, boogers,
5   carpet lice, breadcrumbs. Why don't we ever get to do
6   the fun stuff like those other gnomes?
7 PAT: I don't know. Maybe because we're only gnomes
8   *second-class.* When we get promoted, then we'll get to
9   do some of the funner stuff.
10 JO: Well, I'm tired of these low-life jobs. I'm ready for a good
11   job. I want to be the one who gets to go inside the TV
12   and turn it on and off at odd hours of the night.
13 PAT: Or hide the toothpaste.
14 JO: Or drop pieces of mail behind the refrigerator.
15 PAT: Or steal socks and shorts out of the dirty clothes
16   hamper.
17 JO: Now that's a job to die for!
18 PAT: You're telling me.
19 JO: Yep, that would be the big time.
20 PAT: The only thing better than that is getting to be a yard
21   gnome.
22 JO: That's the pinnacle, all right. I can see it now: Me
23   getting shipped all over the world, and my smiling face
24   — plastered all over the Internet! *(He or she pulls out*
25   *some sunglasses, puts them on, and demonstrates his or her*

9

1 *"photo look."*)
2 PAT: Picture-perfect, dude, picture-perfect. Of course, we
3   could have it worse.
4 JO: Worse? *(Taking off his or her glasses)* What could be worse
5   than this?
6 PAT: Well, we could be toilet gnomes.
7 JO: Oh, geez, you're right about that. Those guys certainly
8   don't get paid enough.
9 PAT: You're telling me. Makes our jobs seem like a breeze.
10   Hey. Here, wanna fresh booger?
11 JO: Thanks. Don't mind if I do. *(Takes a bite.)* Hmmmm.
12   Good.
13 PAT: *(Takes a bite of another booger.)* Yep, A-OK. Just
14   counting my blessings.
15 JO: Yep, counting our blessings. Hey, got any salt on ya?

Assertive

Introduction

We all have the right to stand up for ourselves. In this scene, employee ROBIN and boss PAT stand on opposite sides of a table that has a single cupcake sitting in the middle.

1 PAT: Oh, lookee here. There's one cupcake left! *(PAT starts*
2 *to reach for it. ROBIN fairly jumps over to the cupcake and*
3 *shields it with his or her hand. PAT pulls back.)*
4 ROBIN: Leave it alone. It's mine. Don't touch it.
5 PAT: Excuse me?!
6 ROBIN: I said it's my cupcake. I bought it. I brought it.
7 Leave it alone.
8 PAT: Yeah, but you brought cupcakes for the whole office.
9 That includes me, remember?
10 ROBIN: Yes, I did, and everyone has had one, but me. Now
11 leave that one. It's mine.
12 PAT: I didn't have one.
13 ROBIN: Well, that's too bad. Because ... Look, you're the
14 boss, and I guess you can chew me out and embarrass
15 and humiliate me in front of the whole office anytime you
16 like, and there's nothing I can do to stop you, but this
17 *stinking* cupcake is mine and if you touch it, I swear I'm
18 going to knock you out.
19 PAT: Whoa, wait. Sorry. I didn't mean to make you mad
20 awhile ago in the meeting. I was only trying to make a
21 point. Did I really embarrass you that bad? I mean, I was
22 *only* teasing.
23 ROBIN: Well, let me tell you something, "Boss!" Your
24 comments went way beyond the *(Making quotation marks*
25 *in the air)* "teasing" stage, it went into the *(Making*

11

1   *quotation marks again)* **"harassment" stage. In fact, I**
2   **think ...** *(ROBIN picks up the cupcake and proceeds to peel*
3   *the paper cup.)* **I'm going to march myself down to human**
4   **resources and file a formal complaint against you. You're**
5   **a bully and I'm tired of it.**
6 **PAT: Now, you just hold on just one minute there —**
7 **ROBIN: And this cupcake?** *(ROBIN bites into the cupcake.)* **It's**
8   **mine!**

Calm

Introduction
Sometimes it's almost impossible to stay calm! In this scene, PAT is having a nightmare about diving into a swimming pool full of some really nasty stuff, but thankfully JO is there to help.

1 PAT: I hate this. I hate this. I hate this.

2 JO: Pat, shut up, and try to stay calm.

3 PAT: Stay calm? How can you stay calm? We're fixing to
4   have to swim in a pool full of pus!

5 JO: I know we are. I'm just trying to think our way through
6   this.

7 PAT: It's just a silly game. I didn't know we'd actually have
8   to do this.

9 JO: Take a deep breath, Pat. Relax.

10 PAT: *(In a TV announcer voice)* And the question is: Which
11   would you rather do, suck a dead man's nose or swim in
12   a sea of pus? *(Normal voice)* Well, of course, I picked pus.
13   Everybody picks pus!

14 JO: Pat! Just concentrate. We're gonna get through this.

15 PAT: How? It's pus! It's green! It stinks. And we're
16   supposed to swim a whole lap in it!

17 JO: The quicker we get it done, the quicker it'll be over.

18 PAT: But, I don't want to do this. I repeat: *I don't want to*
19   *do this!*

20 JO: Pat, please. Be calm.

21 PAT: And why are you so calm? Ordinarily, you'd be the one
22   screaming your head off.

23 JO: Well, for one reason, this is your nightmare, not mine.

24 PAT: Oh? Oh, yeah, that's right. This *is* my nightmare. I
25   hate nightmares.

1   JO: **And the second reason is that I get to stay here. You**
2   **don't. Good-bye!** *(JO apparently shoves PAT into the pool.*
3   *PAT disappears Off-Stage.)*
4   PAT: **You what? Aaaawwww!** *(Unseen, from Off-Stage, we hear*
5   *PAT retching. Then weakly)* **I hate this. I soooo hate this.**
6   JO: *(Smiling)* **I know, but you can at least still try to be calm**
7   **about it.**

Confident

Introduction
Confidence can take you a long way; sometimes further! In this scene, daredevil MADISON is preparing to cross the Grand Canyon on a tightrope with the help of assistant BLAIR.

1   BLAIR: You know, it's a five-hundred-foot drop.

2   MADISON: I know. Not a problem.

3   BLAIR: You're crossing the Grand Canyon on a tightrope
4   and you're not worried?

5   MADISON: Nope. I have a show to put on.

6   BLAIR: But how can you not be worried?

7   MADISON: I have supreme confidence in myself. Anything
8   less would be suicide.

9   BLAIR: I see. So, are you? Supremely confident, I mean.

10 MADISON: Of course I am. All the major outlets are here.
11   CNN, NBC, FOX.

12 BLAIR: Well, you're right about that. You're being broadcast
13   all over the world — live!

14 MADISON: Yep. Three hundred million people watching and
15   a one-million-dollar payoff! Do this and I'll never have to
16   work another day in my life.

17 BLAIR: *(Under his or her breath)* If you live another day?

18 MADISON: Whatdya say?

19 BLAIR: Nothing. Nothing. The TV guys are signaling. About
20   time to go.

21 MADISON: Yep. See ya on the other side.

22 BLAIR: Yes, sir. *(Or ma'am)* See you then. *(MADISON exits,*
23   *walking on the tightrope. As he or she does, BLAIR pulls out*
24   *a cell phone and dials. Into phone)* Hello? Hello, Las Vegas
25   odds? What are you laying on him *(Or her)* making it

1   **across? A hundred to one? I'd like to bet fifty thousand.**
2   **Yes, that's right. That he** *(Or she)* **doesn't make it. OK.**
3   **Thanks.** *(Puts phone away. To self)* **Ah, shucks.** I forgot to
4   **tell him** *(Or her)* **about accidently spilling that slick oil on**
5   **the middle of the rope. Oh well. Can't remember**
6   **everything.** *(Calling to MADISON)* **Doing good, Madison!**
7   **MADISON:** *(Off-Stage, calling back)* **Almost halfway across!**
8   **BLAIR:** *(Smiling)* **Yep. Almost ... aaaaal-most.**

Contentment

Introduction
Everybody should be happy with who they are, don't you think? In this scene, we meet PAT and JOE — two pigs in a pigpen — just lying around, enjoying their day.

1 PAT: *(Snorts then chews.)* It's good to be a pig.

2 JOE: *(Snorts.)* Yep. It's fun.

3 PAT: No, I mean this is the best. You look at all the other

4 animals in the barnyard and none of them've got it as

5 good as us. I mean, just think about it. The cows get

6 rounded up every day and Farmer Jones milks 'em.

7 JOE: Yeah. I'd like to see him try that on me. *(Laughs.)* And

8 the chickens? They lay eggs and what happens? Mrs.

9 Jones comes and steals 'em! Oh, brother!

10 PAT: And the horses? They get on them! And then ride

11 around! How humiliating!

12 JOE: When I was younger, that happened to me. It was

13 awful.

14 PAT: Really? Wow. But us? They don't mess with us. They

15 know we're special. They give us slop twice a day and

16 leave us alone to lay in the sun! Now, that's living.

17 JOE: Yep, and I'm working on a beautiful tan.

18 PAT: And mud baths. Oh, yeah, I love my mud baths.

19 JOE: Yep, we got the best of all worlds. *(Munches a little bit.)*

20 You know, the only thing around here I don't like is that

21 awful smell every morning.

22 PAT: What smell?

23 JOE: You haven't noticed? It comes out of Farmer Jones'

24 kitchen window. It smells like they're cooking

25 somebody.

1   PAT: That window over there?

2   JOE: Yeah. Every morning. It stinks.

3   PAT: Oh, that's what *that* is? I wondered.

4   JOE: It's disgusting.

5   PAT: Hey, look, here comes Farmer Jones and his wife.

6   JOE: Oh, look, she's carrying a knife and he's got a gun.

7   Wonder what that's about?

8   PAT: I don't know, but I got a bad feeling we're fixing to find

9   out.

Daring

Introduction
Everybody loves a good dare now and then. In this scene, we find PAT and JO standing on opposite sides of a flagpole in the middle of winter — playing a game of chicken.

1 PAT: If you put your tongue on it, it's going to stick. I saw
2   the movie.
3 JO: Oh, it is not. That's just Hollywood. I heard they used
4   a suction hose.
5 PAT: So? The principle still applies. Haven't you ever stuck
6   to an ice tray?
7 JO: No. My family is rich. We don't use ice trays. We have
8   an icemaker.
9 PAT: Whoopee! Well, one time at my grandma's, I picked up
10   an ice tray with wet hands and my hands stuck! It hurt,
11   too.
12 JO: Fortunately for me, this is a flagpole, not an ice tray.
13 PAT: All right, smart aleck. If you're so right, go ahead!
14   Stick your tongue on it.
15 JO: But what if I don't want to?
16 PAT: What do you mean you don't want to?
17 JO: Well, I never said that I wanted to. We were just having
18   a discussion about it.
19 PAT: You dragged me out of my house and across the street
20   to this stupid flagpole. What do you mean, you don't
21   want to? Ah-ha! The truth comes out. You're afraid to do
22   it!
23 JO: I am not. I was just trying to prove my point.
24 PAT: Then prove it, chicken! Stick your tongue on it! I dare
25   ya. I double dare ya!

1   JO: Now you sound like that kid in the movie. Well ... what
2   am I gonna get for this?
3   PAT: What do you mean "get for this"? If nothing's gonna
4   happen — remember — then why should you get
5   anything?
6   JO: I should get something for going the extra mile to prove
7   you wrong. You think I will. So, what are you going to
8   give me?
9   PAT: I don't know. Oh, how about I take you to McDonald's
10   and buy you anything you want.
11 JO: Anything? And how about as much as I want? Deal?
12 PAT: Yeah-yeah-yeah, deal-deal-deal. Now quit stalling and
13   let's see ya do it! *(Hesitantly, JO moves to the flagpole and*
14   *leans in.)*

Honest

Introduction
Honesty is the best policy. However, in this scene, JO teaches PAT that there may be limits.

1 PAT: Jo, guess what?! I've made a New Year's resolution.

2 JO: Really? And what would that be?

3 PAT: I've resolved to be honest in all my dealing in the
4   upcoming year.

5 JO: Well, that's a noble sentiment as long as you don't carry
6   it too far.

7 PAT: What? What do you mean? How can you carry honesty
8   too far?

9 JO: We all lie to a certain degree all the time. It's called tact.

10 PAT: What do you mean?

11 JO: Well — OK. Let's assume I am completely honest in
12   everything I do.

13 PAT: OK. Fine. Be completely honest.

14 JO: Well ... let's see ... ah ... First off, you've got bad breath.
15   Your hair looks like a rat's nest, and those glasses
16   frames ... aaaagggg!

17 PAT: Hey!

18 JO: Your '82 Nissan? It's a wreck. It's nothing but carbon
19   monoxide poisoning on wheels. I mean, the minute I get
20   *my* car — I'll never ride with you again. Nev-er! It's
21   soooo embarrassing.

22 PAT: Wait a minute! This isn't honesty. This is being just
23   plain cruel!

24 JO: Sweetie, it's both honest *and* cruel. Your clothes are so
25   yesterday, but, hey! What can you expect with re-treads

1   and hand-me-downs? You think you're an *Ellie* model,
2   but you're not! And your signature frog toboggan —
3   PAT: OK, Jo, you can stop now. *Stop!* You've made your
4   point. I get it. I get it. Yes, a person *can* be too honest.
5   Honesty must be tempered with kindness and common
6   sense. Right?
7   JO: Right.
8   PAT: *(A beat)* And you were just making points, right? You
9   didn't *really* mean any of that stuff.
10 JO: *(Rolling his or her eyes as if not sure)* **Weeeellll** —
11 PAT: OK. You can leave now. Honest. I want you to go! Now!
12   Go! I mean it!

Idealistic

Introduction
Knowing history is OK — up to a point! In this scene, we find PAT standing on a chair pontificating loudly as roommate JO enters.

1 PAT: *(Fairly shouting)* "Give me liberty or give me death!"
2 JO: Gee, that's kinda extreme, don't you think?
3 PAT: *(Fairly shouting)* "These are the times that try men's
4   souls."
5 JO: What are you doing?
6 PAT: *(Fairly shouting)* "I regret that I have but one life to give
7   for my country!" *(A bit softer)* It's time to take a stand for
8   the cause!
9 JO: And just exactly *what is the cause?*
10 PAT: Freedom from England! *(Fairly shouting)* "I have not yet
11   begun to fight!"
12 JO: Oh, I see, you are a walking American Revolutionary
13   War quotation book.
14 PAT: *(Normal voice)* Yes, the American Revolution. Freedom
15   for the colonies! Down with tyrants!
16 JO: Uh, Pat, you do know that the American Revolution was
17   two hundred and thirty-five years ago, right? We won
18   that war.
19 PAT: Don't tell me that! I want to be part of the revolt! I
20   want to be idealistic and turn the world upside down! I
21   want to throw tea into Boston Harbor!
22 JO: Sorry, but it's all in the past. *(PAT glares at JO for a
23   second, then looks up thinking, and then)*
24 PAT: *(Fairly shouting)* "With malice towards none and charity
25   towards all."

1 JO: Now that's Lincoln. That's the Civil War.
2 PAT: *(Normal voice)* I'm moving on.
3 JO: Oh, OK, good. Well, let me know when you make it to
4   the twenty-first century. I could use some help cooking
5   supper. *(JO exits. PAT watches JO go and then strikes a new*
6   *pose.)*
7 PAT: The twentieth century: *(Fairly shouting)* "A chicken in
8   every pot, and a car in every backyard!"

Independent

Introduction
We all want to be independent, but that doesn't necessarily mean all the time. In this scene, a very angry JO refuses PAT's help.

1 JO: No! Leave me alone. I can change a tire.

2 PAT: I know you can. I'm just trying to help.

3 JO: Well, maybe I don't want your help. Maybe I've had
4   enough of your help lately.

5 PAT: What does that mean?

6 JO: *Madison!*

7 PAT: Oh. So that's where this is going. *(PAT hands JO the tire*
8   *tool.)*

9 JO: Don't! Don't hand me — I can do this. I'm independent.

10 PAT: Since when? You're a complete klutz. I was just trying
11   to move things along.

12 JO: Yeah? Well, thanks to you, it all just moved right on out
13   the door.

14 PAT: Here, you're not doing those lugs right.

15 JO: *I don't care! I don't care!* Are you not listening to me? I
16   really liked Madison and you messed it up. You messed
17   it up! *You messed it up! (JO kicks the car frame and the car*
18   *falls on JO's leg.)* Awwww!

19 PAT: Oh, no! Here, let me help!

20 JO: No! No! Get away! Don't touch me!

21 PAT: But your leg. It's trapped. Under the car.

22 JO: Oh, is it? You're so smart. Now go away. Leave me
23   alone. Go!

24 PAT: Well, OK. If that's what you really want? *(PAT pulls out*
25   *cell phone and dials a number as he or she walks away.)*

1   Uh — hello? Madison? Hey, what's up? Are you busy
2   tonight? Jo? No, he *(Or she)* is having car problems.

Ingenious

Introduction

Necessity is the mother of invention and hunger is — oh, well, you'll see as in this scene we find classmates PAT and JO discussing the latest discoveries in chemistry.

1 PAT: Then you adjust the flame until it's blue and then you
2   place it above the flame for about one minute and *presto!*
3 JO: That's really ingenious! How long did it take you to
4   figure it out?
5 PAT: Oh, about thirty minutes.
6 JO: Amazing. And Old Man Jones didn't catch you?
7 PAT: Nah. He's in the lunchroom
8 JO: Wow. You are so awesome.
9 PAT: Well, it sure beats the alternative.
10 JO: You're telling me. You waste three-fourths of your lunch
11   period just standing in line.
12 PAT: Not me. I maximized my whole thirty minutes.
13 JO: Do you think you'll be performing this ingenious
14   experiment again anytime soon?
15 PAT: Maybe — if I have a test I'm needing to cram for.
16 JO: Wow. Get the flame blue and then hold it over the
17   burner for one minute? Right?
18 PAT: Yeah, but you got to keep rotating it, and you got to
19   be sure to clean up after yourself so Jones doesn't
20   suspect anything.
21 JO: Naturally. Of course.
22 PAT: And you gotta pack in the other important stuff — you
23   know — like mustard, ketchup.
24 JO: So, you stayed in here the whole lunch period and
25   cooked hotdog weenies over the Bunsen burner?

1   PAT: Yep, and browned my hotdog buns, too.
2   JO: Amazing. Simply amazing.
3   PAT: Yep. Hunger is the mother of invention!

Inquisitive

Introduction
Sometimes, you really don't want to know. In this scene, PAT questions JO about his or her latest heartthrob.

1 PAT: Did he *(Or she)* talk about me? Oh, come on. Give me
2   a little hint.
3 JO: I'm not really at liberty to say. I can't. He *(Or she)* was
4   talking to me confidentially.
5 PAT: OK, I understand that, but you gotta give me a hint.
6   Something! Does he *(Or she)* like me?
7 JO: Well, I guess nothing will be ruined if I tell you that he
8   *(Or she)* spoke positively towards you.
9 PAT: Positive? Good, good. That's good, right?
10 JO: Well, I would think so.
11 PAT: But *how* positive? Positive I'm a nice person or
12   positive he *(Or she)* doesn't want to see me anymore?
13 JO: Now, that part I can't really say.
14 PAT: Why not? You know, don't you?
15 JO: Yes, but that's his *(Or her)* business, not mine. I'm not
16   the go-between here.
17 PAT: Well, you got to tell me something, Jo. You're my best
18   friend. Pleeeease!
19 JO: OK. What do you want to know?
20 PAT: What do I want to know? *You know what I want to*
21   *know!*
22 JO: Well, as I said. He *(Or she)* said some positive things.
23 PAT: What does that mean? What does that mean?
24 JO: I swear. You're the most inquisitive person I've ever
25   met.

1   PAT: Tell me what he *(Or she)* said or I'm going to bust!
2   JO: OK. He *(Or she)* said you were positively one of the
3   nicest people he *(Or she)* has ever met.
4   PAT: And? *And* — ?
5   JO: That was all. That you're a really nice person.
6   PAT: Oh. *(A beat.)* And what do you think that means, huh?
7   "Really nice person"?

Irresponsible

Introduction

Got a job? Be thankful. In this scene, JO finds out that when the boss, PAT, ain't happy, ain't nobody happy!

1 JO: Good morning.

2 PAT: You're late. Forty-five minutes!

3 JO: Sorry. I got stuck in traffic and my cell phone was dead.

4 PAT: This is the seventh time in the last two weeks you've

5   been late.

6 JO: It is? My bad.

7 PAT: Jo, this is not working out. This is a pastry shop. We

8   make our money —

9 JO: *(Finishing the sentence)* "Selling donuts and pastries. If

10   we don't have product for our customers, we don't make

11   money and I can't pay you, and we can't stay open for

12   business."

13 PAT: Then you know how important it is to be on time and

14   to get the donut dough made.

15 JO: Yeah, yeah, yeah.

16 PAT: No, not "yeah, yeah, yeah." How about fired, fired,

17   fired?

18 JO: You can't fire me. You need me!

19 PAT: Not if you're not going to be responsible and make a

20   good employee.

21 JO: I am responsible! Maybe I have been late a little bit

22   lately, but I work my butt off when I'm here!

23 PAT: But your *butt* is never here when I need you.

24 JO: But —

25 PAT: But-but-but-but-*but!* Be late again and you can take

1   your "but" somewhere else.

2 JO: Hmpf! You are so unreasonable!

3 PAT: Blah-blah-blah-blah-blah! *Mix the dough, Jo!* And quit

4   your complaining. *(PAT exits.)*

5 JO: *(Calling after)* Mom! *(Or Dad) (Under his or her breath)* The

6   only reason I work here is because I need some dough.

Knowledgeable

Introduction

Knowledge, as we all know, can come from unexpected sources. This scene demonstrates that point as reporter PAT interviews JO — the most intelligent person in the world.

1   PAT: So, Jo, how does it feel to have won the Nobel Prize in
2   Science six years in a row and to be deemed "The Most
3   Intelligent Person in the World"?
4   JO: Oh, I feel just fine. I had spaghetti and popcorn for
5   lunch, you know.
6   PAT: Spaghetti and popcorn?
7   JO: Yep! We super-smart scientists have to keep our energy
8   up, you know.
9   PAT: Ooookay. So, when did you first form your theory
10   about revolving stars?
11   JO: When I was twenty-two. I was bending over to tie my
12   shoe and fell and hit my head and then I saw all of these
13   little stars revolving around my head.
14   PAT: And that's how ... OK. And your theory of double hex
15   black holes in space?
16   JO: Well, once I was trying to fill a hole in the wall with wood
17   glue and I kept pouring and pouring and pouring and I
18   used three bottles of glue on that hole and it got me
19   thinking.
20   PAT: I see. And your explanation for the Hazy Nebula on the
21   edges of space?
22   JO: Driving home in a fog.
23   PAT: I should have known.
24   JO: Yes, I have figured out a great many things by simply
25   observing the world around me. Birds, the sky, beneath

1   a microscope. Even people at the grocery store. Even

2   you. I've noticed a hair growing off your nose. Here, let

3   me pull it. *(JO tries to pull the hair. PAT moves away.)*

4 PAT: No, no. Leave me alone,

5 JO: No? Alas, another cosmic truth lost to mankind. Oh

6   well, it doesn't matter. I think I made another really

7   important new discovery yesterday.

8 PAT: Yeah, and what might that be?

9 JO: Well, it all started when I was changing my grandson's

10   dirty diaper —

11 PAT: OK. That's enough. I'm outta here. I don't even want

12   to know.

Modest

Introduction

We all know modesty is a virtue, but did you know that sometimes it's expensive? You'll see in this scene as JO, a news reporter, interviews PAT — the world's greatest explorer.

1 JO: It's such an honor to interview you, the world's greatest
2   explorer.
3 PAT: I don't like to brag. I've just been very fortunate really.
4   Very blessed.
5 JO: Here-here! You're just being modest. You've lived an
6   amazing life. Your list of accomplishments takes up
7   three pages.
8 PAT: All in large print, no doubt.
9 JO: It says here you discovered the fountainhead of the
10   Greater Rummy-Woo River.
11 PAT: Blind luck, really.
12 JO: You were the first to climb Mount Waynard.
13 PAT: Owens was ahead of us, of course — until the
14   landslide. Timing is everything.
15 JO: The first westerner to eat gooey-gooey worms with the
16   Mhatti-Mhatti.
17 PAT: Twelve inchers! Tasted like chicken!
18 JO: You endured the winter flatulence of the Southwest
19   Arctic Pass.
20 PAT: Held my breath and just kept going.
21 JO: And it says here you traded toenail clippings with the
22   cannibals of North New Lennex.
23 PAT: It was a house-warming gift, actually. Lots of
24   Tupperware, too. No big deal.
25 JO: My goodness, I can't believe you're so modest about

1   your accomplishments. You even saved the Von Lewis
2   twins!
3 PAT: Yes, but I had good sources. *(A beat)* Is that it? Are we
4   finished? The interview? That's fifteen hundred, please.
5 JO: Excuse me? For what?
6 PAT: My interview fee. Cash or credit?
7 JO: *(A gulp)* Wow, that's a lot of money.
8 PAT: Yep, modesty doesn't come cheap!

Observant

Introduction

They say that not all that glitters is gold. In this scene, LOU, a new astronomy student, demonstrates that truth after peering through Professor DUD's high-powered telescope.

1 LOU: Professor! Professor!

2 DUD: Yes, Lou. What is it?

3 LOU: I think I just made a new discovery!

4 DUD: So soon? My, but you *are* an observant student! It's

5   not often that a student makes a new discovery the first

6   time they look through the telescope.

7 LOU: I think I've discovered a life on Mars!

8 DUD: Really? And how did you do that?

9 LOU: I saw it moving.

10 DUD: Moving? Really?

11 LOU: Look for yourself. *(DUD peers into the telescope and*

12   *screams.)*

13 DUD: Oh, my gosh! It's huge and — and — and hairy and

14   it's got eight legs and it's crawling all over the place.

15 LOU: Yes! Yes! See, I told you!

16 DUD: *(DUD starts jumping around. Screaming)* I've never seen

17   anything like it! Help! Help! We're doomed! We're all

18   going to die!

19 LOU: *(Just as excited)* I don't want to die! Professor, isn't

20   there anything we can do? *(DUD suddenly stops and glares*

21   *at LOU before handing him a handkerchief.)*

22 DUD: *(Matter-of-factly)* Yes! You can take this and go clean

23   that housefly off the telescope lens.

24 LOU: A housefly?

25 DUD: Yes! And then, you can go clean the bathrooms.

Reflective

Introduction

Sometimes it just doesn't pay to think too hard. In this scene, siblings PAT and ROBIN are at the beach. ROBIN, who is into Eastern spirituality, sits in the lotus position on a large rock that juts out into the water. We can hear the ocean wave as PAT climbs onto the rock, too.

1   PAT: Hey, whatchya doin'?

2   ROBIN: I am being one with nature and reflecting on the

3   true meaning of life.

4   PAT: Isn't it a little dangerous to be doing that out here?

5   The waves can come in pretty high.

6   ROBIN: Shhhh. Quiet. You're disrupting my karma. Listen

7   to the waves. *(The loud sound of a wave crashing against*

8   *the rock.)*

9   PAT: Wow! That was a big one! Hey? How come you're not

10   even wet? I'm soaked.

11 ROBIN: Because ... I am *one* with the water. I am one with

12   the universe. Close your eyes and embrace the cosmos.

13   *(The sound of another ocean wave.)*

14 PAT: *Whoa!* That one almost knocked me off the rock.

15   Come on, we better get off of here.

16 ROBIN: *(Meditating)* Hmmmm.

17 PAT: Well, this *one* is leaving.

18 ROBIN: Go on. You're bothering me.

19 PAT: Well, OK, but do be careful.

20 ROBIN: All will be well. *(PAT jumps off the rock and starts*

21   *wading back to shore. The sound of another ocean wave*

22   *coming in. PAT turns around and looks back at ROBIN.)*

23 PAT: Oh, wow, Robin, look! *Watch out! Hurry, get off — !*

24   *(The sound of the ocean waves striking the rock and the*

25   *shore. ROBIN, still sitting calmly, rolls off the rock and*

1   *disappears. PAT runs back towards the rock.)* **Robin?**

2   *ROBIN?* **Where are you?** *ROBIN?* **This is no time to play**

3   **jokes.** *(Listens for a response.)* **If you leave, I'm taking**

4   **your room. I'm going to sell the dog.** *(Listens again.)* **Oh,**

5   **boy. How am I going to explain this one to Mom?**

Relax

Introduction

Do you have fun at the dentist? PAT does! In this scene, you'll see how.

1 PAT: Nurse? I'm really nervous about this. Got anything to
2   help me relax?
3 ROBIN: Yes, right here. What I need you to do is hold this
4   over your face for me and take three deep breaths.
5 PAT: Thanks, you're sure a nice dental hygienist. *(ROBIN*
6   *places the mask over PAT's face. PAT holds it in place as*
7   *ROBIN turns on the gas.)*
8 ROBIN: Thank you. Now, this gas'll relax you. But when you
9   inhale it, don't do it more than three times. Understand?
10   It's pretty powerful stuff. OK? Just three. *No more!*
11 PAT: *(From under the mask)* OK.
12 ROBIN: All right, here we go. Breathe in deep for me. Three
13   times. *(PAT does so, and then ROBIN pulls the mask off*
14   *PAT's face. Off-Stage, a telephone rings.)* Oh, dear, the
15   secretary's out. Hold on. I'll be right back. *(ROBIN exits.*
16   *As soon as ROBIN is gone, PAT throws a glance in ROBIN's*
17   *direction and then takes three more quick breaths, then pulls*
18   *the mask back off his or her face. A moment later, ROBIN*
19   *returns and turns off the gas.)*
20 ROBIN: OK, I'm back. How are we feeling?
21 PAT: Just fine — *(And with that, PAT slips out of the chair and*
22   *slides to the floor. ROBIN gasps in horror and tries to get PAT*
23   *up, but PAT's arms and legs are all rubber. Every time ROBIN*
24   *almost gets PAT back in the chair, PAT slips back down. This*
25   *happens several times to comic effect.)*

1   ROBIN: Oh, oh. I am so sorry. Here, we're almost there.
2   Oops! Sorry. Help me, Pat.
3   PAT: I'm trying, I'm trying. Wow. I feel great. What is that
4   stuff?
5   ROBIN: Not now. Here, I've got to get you up or we're both
6   going to be in trouble. *(Finally, ROBIN works to get PAT*
7   *over his or her shoulder and with great effort puts PAT back*
8   *into the chair to stay.)*
9   PAT: *(Drugged, with slurred speech)* Boy, that was fun! Let me
10   have some more of that stuff.
11 ROBIN: No, no. I think you've had enough.

Responsible

Introduction
In this scene, we join JO, who is babysitting for the first time. Oh, joy! Fun, fun, fun!

1   BO: You're the babysitter. You do it! You're the one getting
2   paid!
3   JO: Hey, but he's *your* little brother!
4   BO: So what? Come on, Getting-Paid-Big-Bucks, change the
5   stupid diaper!
6   JO: But I've never changed one before!
7   BO: I guess it's on-the-job training for you tonight!
8   JO: But what do I do?
9   BO: First, you got to get all the stuff together. Diapers.
10   Baby wipes. Plastic bags.
11   JO: Plastic bags? What do I need plastic bags for? I'm not
12   going to smother him.
13   BO: For putting the diaper in, you dope. *(JO busily gathers*
14   *up all the needed items and returns.)*
15   JO: Oh, OK. Now what?
16   BO: You pull the diaper loose on the sides and raise his legs
17   up. *(JO reaches down and does so and then reacts violently*
18   *at what is seen.)*
19   JO: Oh, my gosh! Now what!
20   BO: Then you take the baby wipes and wipe it until it's
21   clean.
22   JO: Man, I need a shovel or an ice cream scoop or
23   something.
24   BO: Here! Let me do it.
25   JO: I feel sick. You're not going to tell your parents, are you?

1   BO: No, because you're going to give me half of your money,
2   right?
3   JO: *Half of my money!?*
4   BO: Half, or you can do this yourself.
5   JO: Right. Half. Half. It's yours.

Serving

Introduction
If at first you don't succeed, try, try again! Right? In this scene, we find JO, an eager scout, waiting patiently at a street corner for someone to help.

1   JO: I just love being a scout. Being of service and helping
2   people is what I live to do. Oh, look, here comes an itty-
3   bitty old person. *(PAT enters leaning on a walking cane and*
4   *carrying a small bag of groceries. JO approaches.)* **Good,**
5   **morning. How are you? Can I be of assistance? Please,**
6   **take my arm and let me help you cross the street? And**
7   **here, let me carry that bag of groceries for you, too.**
8   *(They start walking.)*
9   PAT: Surely. Thank you. Good to know there's still some
10   nice young people around these days.
11   JO: You're most welcome. It's a nice day, isn't it?
12   PAT: Why yes.
13   JO: Whoa, look out! *Car* — ! *(They both jump back, trip, and*
14   *fall down. JO immediately pops back up and helps PAT to his*
15   *or her feet.)* **Wow. Are you OK?**
16   PAT: Oh, no! *My outfit!* This was the only decent thing I had
17   to wear to my best friend's funeral today, but now it's
18   ruined!
19   JO: I'm sorry.
20   PAT: You know if I hadn't stopped to talk to you, I'd have
21   already been across the street and on the other side and
22   none of this would have happened! Give me back my bag
23   you subversive little whippersnapper and leave me
24   alone!
25   JO: Oh, I hope your eggs aren't broken. If they are, I'll be

1   glad to buy you some new ones.

2   PAT: You can bet your sweet-bippy you will! I'm going to call

3   my lawyer and sue your rear off! *(PAT exits off in a huff.)*

4   JO: But — but — I was only trying to help. Gee, that didn't

5   go too good. Oh well. Here comes somebody else!

6   *(Calling off)* Good morning! How are you? Can I help *you*

7   across the street?

Snooty

Introduction

In this scene, we address the age-old question: Which are better, cats or dogs? As the scene opens, CAT is stretched out on the couch and DOG is busy — as he always is — hopping around.

1   CAT: Oh, you dogs are soooo revolting.

2   DOG: What? What? What? Why ya say that? Why ya say
3   that?

4   CAT: Because you are such easy pushovers. You just throw
5   yourselves at humans.

6   DOG: So? What's wrong with that? That's what people like.
7   They like displays of affection.

8   CAT: But you're *over*-willing. You need to make them work
9   harder for it.

10 DOG: So, what are you saying, huh? Huh? How should I be
11   then? Huh? Huh?

12 CAT: You should be more like a cat. Demure. More self-
13   possessed. More restrained.

14 DOG: Yeah? And what will that get me, huh, huh? What will
15   that get me, huh?

16 CAT: More peace. Plus, they'd appreciate you more when
17   you do *do* something for them.

18 DOG: You said do-do. Haha! That's funny. But everybody
19   loves a friendly dog with —

20 CAT: A wag-a-dy tail and a lick-a-ty tongue. Yes, we know.

21 DOG: You say that like it's a bad thing.

22 CAT: It *is* a bad thing. It's so demeaning. I mean, just look
23   at yourself.

24 DOG: *(Looks at self and likes what he or she sees.)* Yeah. So?

25 CAT: Oh, why do I bother. You'll never understand. You're

1   just a stupid dog.

2   DOG: I am a dog, but I ain't stupid. God put me here to love

3   people and I do.

4   CAT: Don't you realize that loving humans is not that high

5   a calling? Some humans drool! Think about it. *Drooling!*

6   What does that make them? It certainly doesn't make

7   them very high class, does it?

8   DOG: Nope, it sure doesn't. It just makes them cat lovers!

9   CAT: Hey!

10   DOG: Oh, look! Here come the kids again! Hey, guys! Wait

11   for me! *(DOG runs off.)*

12   CAT: *(A beat, then begins licking self)* Oh, please. They're all

13   just soooo disgusting!

Sophisticated

Introduction

Everybody has their standards, right? In this scene, we're back on the farm again as a sophisticated hog argues his or her case for better slop.

1 FARMER: Here you go, Pig. Here's your slop.
2 PIG: *(Sniffs, then turns nose up and moves away.)* Humph!
3 FARMER: What? What's the matter?
4 PIG: You call that slop? That's not slop! That — that —
5   that's trash!
6 FARMER: Trash? No, it's not! All the other hogs like it!
7 PIG: Well, it may work for the other hogs, but I'm a
8   *sophisticated pig!*
9 FARMER: Oh, you are, are you? You're not so sophisticated
10   you don't roll around in the mud.
11 PIG: Yes, but I don't settle for just any old kind of mud,
12   mister! Mine has to be at both the right temperature and
13   the right consistency! *It has to meet A.A.S.P. standards!*
14 FARMER: The A.A.S.P.? What the heck is that?
15 PIG: The American Association of Sophisticated Porcine, of
16   course!
17 FARMER: Oh, brother! If they hear about this at the coffee
18   shop, I'll never live this down.
19 PIG: Tut-tut. Nonsense. Because of me, you're liable to get
20   made farmer of the year!
21 FARMER: Really? Think I'll get my picture in the newspaper
22   or in *Agriculture Today*?
23 PIG: Undoubtedly. We should practice our smile.
24 FARMER: We?
25 PIG: Why, of course. They'll want us *both* in the picture.

48

1   FARMER: Right. Sure. And that's not even mentioning the
2   fact that you're a talking pig!
3   PIG: Nor that *you* talk to a talking pig.
4   FARMER: *(A little concerned)* Oh! ... Yeah ... I hadn't thought
5   of that.
6   PIG: *(Under his breath)* You wouldn't. *(Louder, brighter)* All
7   right, look at the camera. Smile! *(They both strike a pose*
8   *and smile broadly for that future photographer.)*

Superstitious

Introduction

In this scene, we find out that sometimes it just doesn't pay to be too superstitious.

1 BO: Oh, my gosh, I can't believe it! I got *that* close!

2 JO: It's OK. You didn't do anything.

3 BO: Do you — do you know what would have happened if I'd
4   stepped on that crack, Jo?

5 JO: Yes, yes, Bo, you'd have broke your mother's back.

6 BO: I know and I love my mother!

7 JO: I know. I know. It's gonna be OK. *(BO jumps and points*
8   *off into the distance.)*

9 BO: What was that? Oh, no! That was a black cat that just
10   ran across our path! We're doomed!

11 JO: Now, now, I don't think so.

12 BO: Oh, gosh. A crack and now a cat. All this on top of
13   everything else that's happened today.

14 JO: I'm afraid to ask, but what else *has happened* today?

15 BO: I was trying to hang a new mirror in the hall and I
16   dropped it and it broke into a thousand pieces and now
17   I'm going to have —

18 JO: Seven years bad luck! Oh, wow. This *is* getting serious.

19 BO: Help me! What am I going to do?

20 JO: Bo, you know as well as I do that there's only one thing
21   left to do.

22 BO: Jo, you don't mean — ?

23 JO: Yes. *The Wamper!* I have to take a stick and beat you
24   over the head with it. It's the only thing that'll break the
25   spells!

1   BO: Yeah, but The Wamper? Couldn't we do something else?
2   That hurts! I mean, couldn't we just pretend none of
3   this ever happened?
4   JO: Yes, but what would be the fun of that? *(After a moment,*
5   *BO reluctantly nods in agreement and leads the way as they*
6   *exit Off-Stage.)*
7   BO: *(Weakly)* OK. But I get to pick the stick!

Trustworthy

Introduction

In this scene, we find out what real friends are for. JO needs a cigarette and BO can help.

1   JO: OK. Where are they? I need them.

2   BO: Where's *what?*

3   JO: You know, my cigarettes.

4   BO: What cigarettes?

5   JO: The ones I gave you. The ones I gave you — entrusted
6   you — to keep for me.

7   BO: I don't know what you're talking about.

8   JO: Stop! Halt! Time out! Game over. You know perfectly
9   well what I'm talking about. I gave you, the most
10   trustworthy person I know, my pack of cigarettes and
11   told you to keep them from me no matter what and now
12   I want them back. No joking. I need them. *Now!*

13   BO: Really, Jo, I don't know what you're talking about.

14   JO: My smokes! My cigarettes! My cancer sticks! I need
15   them! I got to have my tobacco fix! *Give me the stupid*
16   *smokes!*

17   BO: I don't have the foggiest idea what you're talking about,
18   and besides, if I was doing what you said I'm supposed
19   to be doing, how could I give them back to you? What
20   kind of trustworthy friend would I be then?

21   JO: A good one! A fantastic one! A real lifesaver! Someone
22   who values our friendship. Someone who values my life!
23   *(Threateningly)* Someone who values *their own life!*
24   *(Getting weaker)* Please, please. I beg you. Give me a
25   cigarette.

1 BO: Noooo, no, I don't think so. No cigarettes here. That
2   doesn't sound like a trustworthy friend to me. *(A beat,*
3   *change in attitude)* **How was that?**
4 JO: Pretty good. That was real good. Thanks. Now, give me
5   the pack back.
6 BO: What pack?
7 JO: Bo, don't start this. We were only practicing.
8 BO: Practicing? What practicing? You really *do* want to quit,
9   don't you? *(BO walks away. JO follows.)*
10 JO: Bo, come back here! Bo! *Bo!* Bring me back my stupid
11   cigarettes!

Warm

Introduction

In this scene, CSI members BO and JO discover that the body isn't the only thing warm.

1   BO: The body's still warm.

2   JO: Of course it is. She died on a tanning bed, you idiot!

3   BO: Oh. Oh, yeah.

4   JO: How long has she been dead?

5   BO: Hard to tell. Since she's just warm she may only be

6   half-baked.

7   JO: *(Incredulous)* Riiiight. Speaking of, it sure is warm in

8   here.

9   BO: Oh, here. Let me turn the tanning bed off.

10 JO: Oh, thanks.

11 BO: Don't mention it. *(A beat)* Talking about being warm, did

12   you taste any of Amy's chili?

13 JO: I did and it left a real warm glow in my mouth. Almost

14   like my spilt coffee. It left a real warm glow all over my

15   lap.

16 BO: Ouch. *(A beat)* I know I have never shared this with you,

17   but I think you have a real warm personality.

18 JO: I do? Thanks. How do you know that though?

19 BO: Well, it's simply self-evident.

20 JO: How? You been checking me with a thermometer or

21   something?

22 BO: No, no. Nothing like that.

23 JO: Then how do you know if I have a warm personality?

24 BO: Per-son-ality. Persona. Your character — you project it

25   — you display it by what you do and say. And you come

1   off as a nice, warm person.

2   JO: Well, thanks. You know you're pretty nice yourself!

3   BO: You think? Well, gee, thanks for the compliment. *(They*

4   *hug, then break apart, embarrassed, glance around, and then*

5   *look back down at the body.)*

6   JO: So, this gal. Do you think she had a nice personality?

7   She was still warm when we found her.

Wise

Introduction

You can gain wisdom in the most unlikely places as we'll see in this scene as a seeker of truth, STU, short for student, questions The WISE One on top of a far eastern Tibetan mountaintop.

1 STU: Oh, Great and Wise One, how can I learn the meaning
2   of life?
3 WISE: Watch *The Three Stooges!* To learn the great truths,
4   think "What would Moe do?"
5 STU: *The Three Stooges?* I don't understand. What do you
6   mean?
7 WISE: OK. Here, lean towards me. *(STU leans forward.)* Now
8   if I were Moe, what would I do?
9 STU: I don't know.
10 WISE: He'd do this. *(WISE whacks STU's head with the base of*
11   *his or her hand's palm.)*
12 STU: Aaaa-ooooow! That hurt. *(WISE makes a fist with that*
13   *same hand.)*
14 WISE: Now hit my hand. *(STU makes a fist and hits the top of*
15   *WISE's hand. WISE's hand flies around and strikes STU on*
16   *top of his or her head.)*
17 STU: Hey! Stop that!
18 WISE: See. That's what Moe would do. So, what do you do
19   when you're around a "Moe"?
20 STU: Well, I'm sure not going to allow myself to be in that
21   situation again.
22 WISE: And if I make hooks out of my fingers? *(WISE makes*
23   *hooks out of two of his or her fingers and reaches out towards*
24   *the underside of STU's nose. STU quickly covers his or her*
25   *nose with his or her hand and moves away.)*

1   STU: I'd get the heck away.
2   WISE: See, you're getting smarter already!

Male and Female

*Roles written for
a male and a female*

Abusive

Introduction
Child abuse is a crime. If you're in it, tell somebody you trust. Get help! If you're aware of it, report it. In this scene, JUNE's inebriated DAD attempts to continue abusing her.

1   DAD: *(Slurring his speech)* **Thought you'd tell that silly**
2   **counselor lady, didn't ya?**
3   **JUNE: No, Daddy, I didn't tell anybody.** *(DAD swings the belt*
4   *at her legs. She tries to escape.)*
5   **DAD: Oh, yeah? Then how come I got a call today, huh?**
6   **JUNE: I don't know.** *(DAD swings at her again, but she dodges*
7   *the blow.)*
8   **DAD: You don't know? You'd better know! What'd you do?**
9   **Tell one of your loudmouth friends?**
10 **JUNE: No, I didn't tell anybody. Really.**
11 **DAD: Then why'd they ask me a bunch of questions about**
12   *some* **bruises, huh?**
13 **JUNE: It must have been the school nurse.**
14 **DAD: What?**
15 **JUNE: Emily Johnson was sick so I went with her to the**
16   **nurse's office, and when I helped her lie down, my shirt**
17   **shifted or something and the nurse saw my bruises.**
18 **DAD: And you told her what? That I gave those to you?**
19 **JUNE: No, Daddy.** *(The doorbell rings.)*
20 **DAD:** *(Angrily)* **Who the hell is that?** *(DAD glares at JUNE.*
21   *Then silently, she crosses to a chair and gathers up her*
22   *sweater from off the back of it as if she is about to leave the*
23   *room. She then looks at her father.)*
24 **JUNE: It's the police, Daddy. I called them.**
25 **DAD:** *(Stammering)* **Why-why-why-why-why-why-what did you**

1   do that for?

2 JUNE: Because you can't hit me anymore, Daddy. I'm not

3   going to let you.

Accepting

Introduction
It's good to be accepting of others, but maybe not always. In this scene, good ol' ADAM and EVE are about to make an unexpected discovery!

1 ADAM: So, let me get this straight. The snake gave you this
2   apple?
3 EVE: Yes.
4 ADAM: And because he gave it to you, you ate it?
5 EVE: Yes.
6 ADAM: Why did you do that?
7 EVE: Well, because he was so nice about it and seemed to
8   have my best interest at heart.
9 ADAM: So, you're just very accepting of people, or should I
10   say of snakes?
11 EVE: Well, that's true. I am very accepting of people — you
12   actually — you're the only people here and then all the
13   animals. They've all been just so nice and everything
14   since I got here. I've just never seen any reason not to
15   be accepting. Have you?
16 ADAM: Since you put it like that, uh, no. Not really. So, was
17   it any good? The apple, I mean?
18 EVE: I thought it was. I'd recommend it. Here, try a bite.
19 ADAM: Well, since I do respect your opinion, and you've
20   never given me any reason not to accept your
21   recommendations — *(EVE gives ADAM the apple and he*
22   *takes a bite out of it.)*
23 EVE: Of course not. *I am a woman.* I have good taste and a
24   high fashion sense.
25 ADAM: *(Chewing)* Hmmmm. This is pretty good.

1 EVE: I thought you'd like it.

2 ADAM: Goodness, my head's spinning a little. *(A beat, he*

3   *looks her over.)* Whoa, wow. Where'd you get that outfit?

4 EVE: Get my outfit? I bought it — whoa! Wait a minute. I

5   don't have an outfit. I'm naked!

6 ADAM: And you know what? I am, too.

7 EVE: Uh-oh, I think we just got ourselves into some big

8   trouble.

9 ADAM: Oh, boy! The Big Guy's not going to like this!

Adaptable

Introduction

Once again, we see how adaptation is necessary for the survival of the species. Watch as BOB adapts to his changing dating landscape.

1 BOB: I am so excited about seeing *The Expendables*.
2   Thanks for coming with me, Marlene.
3 MARLENE: Baby, would you mind if we didn't go see *The*
4   *Expendables?* It's not really my kind of movie. Could we
5   go see *Eat Pray Love* instead? Please, please, with sugar
6   on top.
7 BOB: But you knew what movie I wanted to come see before
8   we came. *(Sighing)* **Oh, OK.** *(To the ticket seller)* **Two**
9   tickets to *Eat Pray Love* please.
10 MARLENE: You're so sweet. *(MARLENE kisses BOB on the*
11   *cheek as they walk into the theatre and move to the*
12   *concession stand.)*
13 BOB: No, I'm not. I'm a sucker. *(To the concession worker)*
14   The Giant Pack, please — with a Coke. And butter on
15   the popcorn, please.
16 MARLENE: No, no! No butter. No butter. Honey, that butter
17   is a heart killer. *(To the concession worker)* **And make that**
18   a Diet Coke.
19 BOB: But I like butter.
20 MARLENE: But all the cholesterol! Do you want to fall over
21   dead from a heart attack! *(A beat)* **Oh, look, there's Sally**
22   and Sue!
23 BOB: *(Incredulous)* **Oh, great. The Gabby Sisters.**
24 MARLENE: I told them we'd meet them here and all go to
25   the movies together.

1   **BOB: You told them?** *You told them?!*

2   **MARLENE: Why sure. You don't mind, do you?**

3   **BOB:** *(Looks at her for a long moment, then)* **No, no, I "don't**

4   **mind." And the reason I "don't mind" is because ... our**

5   **date is now officially over. In fact,** *all* **our dating is over.**

6   **Go play with your friends.** *(BOB takes her by the shoulders*

7   *and pushes her off in the direction of her friends. Letting out*

8   *a "huff," she throws a disbelieving glance back at him as she*

9   *marches off to her friends. To concessions worker)* **Sir? Sir?**

10   **If you don't mind, I would like butter on my popcorn,**

11   **please. Thanks.**

Argumentative

Introduction
In this scene, we find DORIS arguing with her husband, BILL — again! This time though, BILL's just cut down the apple tree their granddaughter gave them as a gift.

1   DORIS: I should punch your eyes out.

2   BILL: It was just a tree.

3   DORIS: An apple tree! Given to us — in case you forgot —

4   by our granddaughter!

5   BILL: But Doris, *I'm* a pecan man.

6   DORIS: Bill, you have six pecan trees in the backyard

7   already! You don't need another one.

8   BILL: But this one's a new variety.

9   DORIS: But you already have six pecan trees in the

10   backyard.

11 BILL: Now we have seven.

12 DORIS: And who's going to explain this to our

13   granddaughter?

14 BILL: I bet she won't even notice.

15 DORIS: *But* when she does, who's going to explain it to her?

16   (*A long moment — a standoff.*)

17 BILL: You're pressing your luck, Doris.

18 DORIS: No, you are.

19 BILL: Doris!

20 DORIS: Bill!

21 BILL: Doris!

22 DORIS: Bill!

23 BILL: That's it!

24 DORIS: What? What do you want? Wanna fight? Huh, do

25   you?

1   BILL: Darn right! Bring it on, Doris!

2   DORIS: No, you take it out, Bill! Outside! Here's your pillow.

3   Go sleep with your tree!

Beautiful

Introduction

In this scene, we find out whether using the "right" word is really important or not as PAT's dreamy homage to her latest heartthrob gets abruptly interrupted by her brother, JOE.

1 JOE: What do you mean "He's so beautiful"? He's a guy. He
2   can't be beautiful.
3 PAT: Yes, he can. I think he's beautiful!
4 JOE: "Beautiful" is a feminine term. He can be "handsome"
5   or "good-looking," but he can never be *(Says the*
6   *following in a mock girlie voice)* "beautiful."
7 PAT: Yes, he can. You just don't understand! He's perfect.
8   He's sixteen, and sings love songs like a god. He's all
9   male ... and he's beautiful ... And he's mine. All mine.
10 JOE: Oh, brother. *Girls!* You're all crazy.
11 PAT: Well, who do you think's beautiful?
12 JOE: _____ *(Insert name of latest female heartthrob).*
13   Now, that's one beautiful babe.
14 PAT: Only because her bust has its own zip code!
15 JOE: Noooo, it's not! It's her hair! Her eyes! Not to mention
16   her personality! Besides, when she smiles into the
17   camera, it's just like she's smiling right at me.
18 PAT: Oh, brother! You are such a liar. None of my friends
19   think she's pretty at all. You guys are just all boob
20   maniacs.
21 JOE: Well, at least we're smart enough to not go around and
22   call guys *beautiful!*
23 PAT: If you were a girl, you'd understand.
24 JOE: I don't care, I just hope that when you finally get a *real*
25   boyfriend I'm around *(In a faux French accent)* when he

1   leans over to you and says, "Pat, bay-bee, you are so ...

2   so handsome!" *(Laughs.)*

3   PAT: Shut up! Shut up! *(Calling off)* Mom! Joe's bothering

4   me!

5   JOE: And do you know why I hope I'm around to hear that?

6   Because *nobody* is ever going to tell you you're —

7   *beautiful!* *(JOE runs off laughing.)*

8   PAT: Joe, I hate you! Come back here! You're gonna get it!

Betrayed

Introduction

Being dumped is never easy. Just ask JAYMIE. As the scene begins, she's just climbed into the cab of her boyfriend's pickup on what she thinks is going to be a hot date.

1　JAYMIE: So, honey, where are we going tonight?

2　RICHARD: Oh, I thought that we'd just sit out here in the

3　　driveway and do some heavy petting.

4　JAYMIE: Excuse me? I thought we were going to the movies.

5　RICHARD: Well, we would, but the fact is ... I'm a little short

6　　on cash.

7　JAYMIE: Richard! You just got paid last week.

8　RICHARD: I know, I know ... but ... well ... I've kinda sorta

9　　spent it already.

10　JAYMIE: Kinda sorta? What do you mean "spent it already"?

11　　*On what?*

12　RICHARD: Wanda.

13　JAYMIE: Wanda. *Wanda?* Who in the world is *Wanda?*

14　RICHARD: She's my manatee.

15　JAYMIE: Your *manatee?*

16　RICHARD: Yeah. She surfaced in our lake a couple of weeks

17　　ago, and I kinda started taking care of her and well ...

18　　one thing just led to another, and now — well — well —

19　　we're an item!

20　JAYMIE: Whoa! You're an item? *With a manatee?* Wait a

21　　minute! Are you telling me that I'm being dumped for a

22　　fish? And — and that you spent all your money on — ?

23　　Richard! How in the world do you spend fifteen hundred

24　　dollars on a stupid *sea cow?*

25　RICHARD: Well, I didn't intend to. It just kinda happened. I

1 mean, by the time you figure in the gas and the eats ...
2 and the T-shirts —
3 JAYMIE: T-shirts? *What T-shirts?*
4 RICHARD: The ones we got at Sea World. *(JAYMIE glares at*
5 *RICHARD for a long moment before bailing out of the truck.)*
6 JAYMIE: That's it! Good-bye. I'm outta here.
7 RICHARD: Jaymie, no! Wait! If you'll only meet her!

Caring

Introduction
In this scene, we look in on Little BO Peep and Little JACK Horner and find out that not all is well even in Nursery Rhyme Land.

1 BO: You don't care how I feel. If you cared, you'd treat me
2   with more respect.
3 JACK: Of course I care. I don't know what else you want
4   from me. I invited you to play in my rain barrel.
5 BO: Yes, but you didn't invite me to slide down your cellar
6   door!
7 JACK: I know, I know. I just forgot. I'm sorry.
8 BO: How are we supposed to be "jolly friends forevermore"
9   if you don't invite me to do everything?
10 JACK: Bo, sweetie, I just wasn't thinking.
11 BO: You know how the song goes, Jack.
12 JACK: Yeah, yeah.
13 BO: So?
14 JACK: *(Sighs, then sings.)*
15   Come play in my rain barrel
16   slide down my cellar door
17   and we'll be jolly friends
18   forevermore.
19 BO: *(A beat, then)* No!
20 JACK: Excuse me?
21 BO: No. I don't want to. You didn't do it because you wanted
22   to. You did it 'cause I begged.
23 JACK: No, that's not true.
24 BO: But Jack, what's a girl to do? I need to know you care
25   about me.

1   JACK: Alice, I do care about you. *(A beat, trying to recover)* I
2   mean Bo.
3   BO: Alice? Did you just call me *Alice?* Oh, now I get it.
4   You've been sneaking around with that Wonderland chick
5   again, haven't you? *(JACK throws up his hands in defeat*
6   *and exits Off-Stage. BO is right behind him.)* Jack Horner!
7   Don't you walk away from me! Do you hear me? Come
8   back here! You've got some explaining to do!

Clever

Introduction

Sometimes, you know, it just doesn't pay to be too clever. As the scene opens, we find SHELIA holding a plate of cookies and watching her brother BOB, sporting a magician's cape and hat, who has just finished performing his latest magic trick.

1 BOB: Ta-daaaa!

2 SHELIA: Yeah, bro, that's pretty clever. So, what else can

3   you do?

4 BOB: Oh, that's the only trick I've got down so far, but I'm

5   practicing on some others.

6 SHELIA: *(Skeptical)* Uh-huh. Here. Want a cookie? *(BOB*

7   *helps himself to a half dozen cookies and wolfs them down*

8   *as they talk.)*

9 BOB: Pretty soon I'm going to be the cleverest person at

10   Elroy D. Jones High School — in the whole town maybe.

11 SHELIA: You think? Maybe.

12 BOB: How can you say "maybe"? Who do you know who's

13   cleverer than me?

14 SHELIA: There is no such word as clever-er.

15 BOB: Yes, there is. Looked it up in the dictionary. See, you

16   don't know everything.

17 SHELIA: I never claimed that I did. You're the one who's

18   always trying to be clever.

19 BOB: And for good reason. Things are different with boys.

20   More is expected of us. We have to be clever. To get by

21   in the world! To make our way! To find a mate!

22 SHELIA: Oh, good grief. The only girl who'll marry you will

23   have to be — oh, nevermind.

24 BOB: Na-na-na-na. You're just jealous 'cause I'm clever

25   and you're not.

1   SHELIA: Oh, I wouldn't say that.

2   BOB: Oh, yeah? What have you ever done that was clever?

3   Huh?

4   SHELIA: Well, I laced these cookies with two bars of

5   chocolate ex-lax!

6   BOB: *You did what!?* You mean — ? Oh ... oh ... Oh, noooo!

7   *(BOB grabs his stomach and frantically rushes Off-Stage.)*

8   SHELIA: *(Calling after him)* Hey! Don't forget to practice while

9   you're in there!

Committed

Introduction
In this scene, from the darkened backseat of a car on Lover's Lane, JO explains to PAT the facts about — not the birds and the bees — the chickens and the pigs.

1   JO: You're a chicken.

2   PAT: What? I'm not chicken. I'm willing to do this.

3   JO: No, I didn't say you were chicken. I said you were *a*
4   chicken!

5   PAT: What does that mean?

6   JO: It means you're a chicken and you expect me to be a
7   pig.

8   PAT: A pig? What are you talking about?

9   JO: Breakfast. Breakfast! Ham and eggs! Breakfast! Don't
10   you get it? You're the chicken and I'm the pig. You're
11   involved in breakfast, but I'm the one who has to be
12   committed.

13 PAT: Committed? What are you talking about?

14 JO: Pat, don't be so dense. I thought you said you loved me.

15 PAT: I did. I do, Jo. That's why I want to make love to you.

16 JO: But what does that mean to you, huh? Doesn't love
17   mean wanting what's best for the other person? Well,
18   what if we do this thing and I get pregnant? Then what?
19   Are you still going to love me then and be committed to
20   me or are you just going to walk away?

21 PAT: Whoa — you're getting way ahead of things. *(A break)*
22   I brought a condom.

23 JO: And you wanna play chicken.

24 PAT: Wait, wait, wait. I don't get this chicken business.

25 JO: At breakfast, you can have ham and eggs. To get eggs,

1   a chicken lays it, but then she can just walk away! To
2   get bacon, a pig has to be committed! She has to die!
3   That's the point: There's no getting out of it. If I get
4   pregnant, you can walk away, *I can't!*
5 PAT: Well, if that happens, I guess I could marry you. *(A*
6   *beat)* Or you could get an abortion.
7 JO: *(She glares at him, then)* OK. That's it. Take me home!
8   Now I'm really mad! If I'm gonna throw seventy-five per
9   cent of my life choices out the window in one fell swoop,
10   I'm not going to do it with you. Take me home. *Now!*
11 PAT: Oh, brother. I knew this wasn't going to work out.

Dynamic

Introduction

Don't you hate it when you get a speech stuck inside your head? In this scene, the PRESIDENT and his SPOUSE get ready for a nice romantic White House dinner.

1 PRESIDENT: *(Speaks in a loud, speech-giving voice*
2   *throughout)* **Honey, I'm home.**
3 SPOUSE: Oh, good dear, how was your day?
4 PRESIDENT: Wonderful. I spoke to congress, the NAACP,
5   and to almost three hundred million of my fellow
6   Americans by way of TV.
7 SPOUSE: I know. So, in celebration, I sent the chef on
8   home tonight and cooked dinner for us.
9 PRESIDENT: You did what?
10 SPOUSE: I cooked dinner. So we could have an evening to
11   ourselves. I cooked your favorite.
12 PRESIDENT: You did? You did? What did you cook?
13 SPOUSE: Let me give you a hint. It comes from a country
14   that has a leaning tower.
15 PRESIDENT: Oh, I know what country that is! My fellow
16   Americans, I come before you tonight with an important
17   matter.
18 SPOUSE: Oh, I always love it when you talk like that. Do it
19   again. Do it again!
20 PRESIDENT: My fellow Americans, I've been the leader of
21   the free world all day today, but tonight, I'm eating
22   Italian food with my spouse!
23 SPOUSE: Oh, you sexy thing. I love it when you talk like
24   that. You're so dynamic!
25 PRESIDENT: Yes, I am! And when I put the whole force of

1   my will and personality behind my words, I move
2   mountains and change lives.
3 SPOUSE: Oh, and speaking of changing. You'll need to
4   change clothes so you don't spill any of my great, cheesy
5   *spaghetti* on that lovely Armani suit that nice lobbyist
6   gave you.
7 PRESIDENT: You cooked spaghetti?
8 SPOUSE: Uh-huh! Your favorite!
9 PRESIDENT: You know it, baby! *(Singing to the tune of "God*
10   *Bless America")* God bless spa-ghet-a-tee! Food that I
11   love!
12 SPOUSE: Oh, I love it when you sing that.
13 PRESIDENT: I know, baby, I know!

Embarrassing

Introduction
Oh boy, some crimes really do cause a big stink. In this scene, we find PAT, a security guard at Tiffany's in New York, has just taken ROBIN, a customer, into custody.

1　PAT: Have a seat, ma'am. I'm calling the police.

2　ROBIN: The police? Why? I don't understand. I didn't do
3　　anything.

4　PAT: *(Into phone)* NYPD? Tiffany's. Agent four-three-five-six.
5　　We have a forty-four-forty-nine. *(Listens, then)* OK.
6　　Thanks.

7　ROBIN: I was just standing there and suddenly you guys
8　　came rushing at me. Four of you!

9　PAT: You were standing next to the Tiffany Diamond
10　　display.

11　ROBIN: Yeah. So?

12　PAT: You were standing there all alone. *For a long time!*
13　　That's a sign that you're about to try *something* — like
14　　stealing the diamond!

15　ROBIN: I wasn't going to steal the diamond. I was just
16　　standing there.

17　PAT: So you say. You can explain it to the judge. You looked
18　　suspicious and it's our job to protect the diamond. We
19　　take no chances.

20　ROBIN: Oh, I see. But I only moved over there to get away
21　　from everybody in my group.

22　PAT: Get away? Why? Why'd you want to get away from your
23　　group? And don't lie to me, miss! My patience is wearing
24　　a little thin with you.

25　ROBIN: Well, it's because ... I ... uh ... you know ... passed

1   some gas and I was embarrassed.

2 PAT: You mean to tell me you moved over there to hide a

3   stinky toot?

4 ROBIN: Yes, sir. *(PAT retrieves his cell phone and re-dials.)*

5 PAT: Oh, brother. *(Talks into the phone)* **NYPD? Tiffany's.**

6   Agent four-three-five-six. Cancel that forty-four-forty-nine

7   I just called in. It was only a two-two-two. *(Listens, then)*

8   Yeah. Sorry. Thanks.

9 ROBIN: Excuse me, but did you just use a code number for

10   "passing gas"?

11 PAT: Yes, ma'am. We're professionals! We've got a code for

12   everything.

13 ROBIN: *(Impressed)* **Really? Wow.** *(Changing the subject)* **May**

14   **I go now?**

Equalizing

Introduction
The guy in this scene has a disarming charm about him. Ah, more adventures in dating!

1   DOLORES: This is an awkward thing to say, but I've never
2   dated a one-armed guy before.
3   HERMAN: And is that going to be a problem?
4   DOLORES: No, no. It just seemed like it might be the
5   proverbial elephant in the room that everyone ignores,
6   and I didn't want to do that so I thought I might just get
7   it out of the way.
8   HERMAN: Well, I think that's pretty sensible and I admire
9   you for saying it.
10 DOLORES: I'm embarrassed for having said it. But, I ... Is
11   it a real inconvenience?
12 HERMAN: Oh, sure. Of course it is. We live in a two-armed
13   world. But, it hasn't slowed me down that much. I can
14   still do most everything I want.
15 DOLORES: That's good. I can't even imagine how life would
16   be without one of my arms.
17 HERMAN: Really? Well, let's give try it, whatdaya say?
18 DOLORES: What do you mean? *(HERMAN whips out a roll of*
19   *duct tape.)*
20 HERMAN: Here, pull out the end of this and now stick it to
21   your shirt right here and hold it and put your left arm
22   down against your side. *(DOLORES does and HERMAN*
23   *encircles her with tape and pins her left arm against her*
24   *body.)* There you go. Now you look just like me.
25 DOLORES: *(A little shocked)* My goodness. I do, don't I?

1   Wow. Ha! I'm — I'm one-armed.

2   HERMAN: Yep. Best looking one-armed woman I've seen all

3   year.

4   DOLORES: *(Surprised, flattered)* Really? Am I?

5   HERMAN: Without any doubt. Now we're ready to go. Here,

6   let me hold the door open for you. And you know what?

7   I've discovered there's lots of great things you can do

8   that don't require two arms.

9   DOLORES: *Ooooh, really?* Oh, wow, maybe later ... you can

10   show me some!

11 HERMAN: Absolutely! *(They exit.)*

Grotesque

Introduction
In this scene, QUASIMODO has just rescued ESMERALDA from an angry crowd and swept her up to the bell tower of Notre Dame. He has saved her life. She is about to change his.

1 ESMERALDA: *(Breathless)* **You saved me! From the mob.**
2 **You risked your life! Why?** *(QUASIMODO glances up at her,*
3 *but then looks away and moves off. He stares out into space*
4 *for a long time. Finally)*
5 QUASIMODO: *(Muttering, low)* **You are beautiful.** *(A beat)* **I**
6 **could not stand to see such beauty destroyed.**
7 *(ESMERALDA moves closer to hear him better. He*
8 *instinctively moves away from her.)*
9 ESMERALDA: **Ohhhh, you poor sweet soul!**
10 QUASIMODO: **Go away! I didn't save you to torment me!**
11 **Don't! Don't look at me. I'm ugly. I'm grotesque.**
12 ESMERALDA: **You poor creature. I see nothing grotesque**
13 **here. I see a ... a beautiful soul.** *(QUASIMODO grunts and*
14 *moves away from her. As he stares down at the crowd below,*
15 *he wipes tears from his eyes.)*
16 QUASIMODO: **Bah! Such words!** *(A beat)* **I'm in trouble. The**
17 **Masters are going to beat me.**
18 ESMERALDA: **Please. Let me show you my gratitude. I owe**
19 **you my life.** *(She goes to touch him, but he waves his arms*
20 *violently at her and moves away.)*
21 QUASIMODO: **No. Don't touch me! That would be**
22 **unbearable!**
23 ESMERALDA: **Unbearable? Why?**
24 QUASIMODO: **Have you no mercy? No one has ever**
25 **touched me. To be touched means to be loved. And no**

1   **one has ever loved me!** *(ESMERALDA moves closer to*
2   *QUASIMODO. He grimaces and turns his back to her, but she*
3   *slowly puts her arms around him.)*
4   **ESMERALDA:** *(Tenderly)* **No, not no one.** *(QUASIMODO sobs*
5   *while held in her arms. ESMERALDA strokes his hair.)*

Loyal

Introduction
In this scene, we find out from HERMAN and LILY that even *true love* has its limits.

1 HERMAN: Will you always love me?

2 LILY: Yes.

3 HERMAN: Will you always be loyal to me?

4 LILY: Absolutely.

5 HERMAN: Will you never leave me?

6 LILY: Never.

7 HERMAN: Even though the house is burning down around

8   us?

9 LILY: It is?

10 HERMAN: Yes.

11 LILY: Well, there are limits.

12 HERMAN: Look! My foot is stuck in this crack and I can't

13   get it out and I know I'm doomed. I'll either die from

14   asphyxiation or be burned alive like Joan of Arc. Will you

15   stay here with me?

16 LILY: I'll stay as long as I can. They don't call me Loyal Lily

17   for nothing.

18 HERMAN: But will you stay and perish with me?

19 LILY: Didn't you hear me? I'm Loyal Lily, not Stupid Lily!

20 HERMAN: You're going to desert me!

21 LILY: Well, maybe later, but I'm here right now.

22 HERMAN: OK. Hold my hand. *(She does and he immediately*

23   *handcuffs her to himself.)* **Now we'll go together.**

24 LILY: Maybe you will, but lucky for me, I've got my handy-

25   dandy combination electric saw chain cutter. Bye. *(She*

1   *cuts the chain on the handcuffs and gets up and exits.)*

2   **HERMAN: Lily? You're coming back, aren't you?** *(A beat)*

3   **Lily?** *(Calling)* **It's getting warm in here!**

Modesty

Introduction

In this scene, we find out that when it comes to modesty, it's not always what you think.

1   GINA: I can't believe you saw me naked! Why'd you walk in
2   on me like that?
3   BOB: Sorry. I didn't know you were in there.
4   GINA: You didn't hear the shower?
5   BOB: Obviously not, Gina!
6   GINA: You got your eyes full, didn't you, Bob? Don't deny it.
7   I saw you staring at *them!*
8   BOB: But it wasn't intentional. I mean — I just opened the
9   door and there you were and there *they* were!
10 GINA: I am so embarrassed. You stared at them!
11 BOB: Yes! OK? I stared at them, I admit it! How could I not?
12   They're so beautiful!
13 GINA: My modesty has never been so invaded! I feel so
14   violated.
15 BOB: But you shouldn't. They're beautiful. They're the most
16   beautiful pair of —
17 GINA: No! Don't say it. Don't you dare say it!
18 BOB: But I have to! They're the most beautiful pair of — of
19   — *ankles* I've ever seen!
20 GINA: *No!* Stop it! I'm covering up my ears!
21 BOB: The way they protrude out from the rest of your leg.
22   So smooth. So curvy.
23 GINA: *You. Shut. Up.* I am not just a pair of ankles! I'm a
24   person.
25 BOB: I know. But they're still a beautiful part of you.

1   GINA: A very *private* part of me.

2   BOB: OK! Look. It happened. It's over. I'm sorry. It'll never

3   happen again.

4   GINA: No, that's not good enough. If you get to see mine,

5   then I ought get to see yours! Even Steven! So, I want

6   to see *yours!* Right now! So, drop the pants!

7   BOB: Whoa — now wait a minute! Mine was an accident!

8   GINA: Well, mine's not! So unzip 'em Bob and drop 'em! *I*

9   *wanna see those knees!*

Powerful

Introduction
In this scene, Captain DYNAMO, the world's most powerful man, meets his match when CHELSEA, an adoring fan, hands him a certain little bundle.

1   DYNAMO: There! Once again, I, Captain Dynamo, have
2   pulled a twenty-ton train fifty yards with my bare teeth.
3   CHELSEA: Oh, Captain Dynamo, you're so wonderful!
4   DYNAMO: Yes, I am. The most powerful force on earth.
5   CHELSEA: Well, not exactly.
6   DYNAMO: Yes, well — huh!? Excuse me. Who's more
7   powerful than me?
8   CHELSEA: Clarence.
9   DYNAMO: Clarence? Who in the world is *Clarence?*
10 CHELSEA: My one–year-old.
11 DYNAMO: Your —
12 CHELSEA: One-year-old. He poops. He cries. He wails. He
13   is a force to be reckoned with.
14 DYNAMO: He's a baby, for crying out loud. No pun intended.
15   He can't do anything.
16 CHELSEA: You know, you're right. Here. I'm going to the
17   bathroom. *(She hands him her bundled-up baby and exits.)*
18 DYNAMO: What?! Whoa, ma'am, ma'am? *(To the baby)* Huh,
19   hi there ... Clarence. *(A loud noise. DYNAMO starts*
20   *switching the baby bundle from arm to arm.)* Oh, kid, you
21   didn't poop, did you? Oh, yuck. No, it's dripping out.
22   Rats! On my new outfit! *(A beat)* Oh, no. Kid! Throw up!
23   Oh, yuck. Yuck. *(Another loud noise. CHELSEA reenters.*
24   *DYNAMO hands the baby back to her.)*
25 CHELSEA: So, how's it going?

1   **DYNAMO: Here, take him, lady. I give up. He wins. Yuck.**

2   *(DYNAMO walks off while trying to fling poop off his fingers.)*

Quiet

Introduction
In this scene, BO and JO, an old couple, sit side by side on a porch swing. Your challenge as an actor for this scene is to fill in the silences with meaning.

1   JO: You haven't said anything in awhile.

2   BO: Just sitting quiet.

3   JO: OK. *(BO gazes at JO for a long moment and smiles. She*

4   *turns and sees him looking at her. She smiles back. He*

5   *reaches out and she takes his hand and they hold hands.)*

6   BO: It's a pretty sunset.

7   JO: Yep. *(A silence between them.)*

8   BO: There's some fireflies.

9   JO: I love fireflies.

10 BO: Me too. *(Another silence.)*

11 JO: Can you smell the honeysuckle?

12 BO: Mmmmhmmmm. Listen. *(They listen for a moment.)*

13 JO: Crickets.

14 BO: Yep. Feel that breeze?

15 JO: It's nice.

16 BO: Good sleeping tonight.

17 JO: Good snuggling weather.

18 BO: Ready to go in?

19 JO: When you are.

20 BO: I am. Let's go.

Shocking

Introduction

In this scene, ROBIN opens her front door to find PAT, her date, standing on the front porch dressed as a frog. More shocking revelations follow.

1 ROBIN: *Pat!* What are you doing? I am shocked!

2 PAT: No, you're not. Not 'til you shake my hand. Put-er

3   there! *(PAT sticks out his hand to shake. ROBIN takes his*

4   *hand, screams, and recoils in pain.)*

5 ROBIN: *Aaaahhhh!*

6 PAT: Now you've been shocked. *(ROBIN rubs her throbbing*

7   *hand as PAT shows her the little hidden palm device.)*

8 ROBIN: What was that?

9 PAT: Just my little handy-dandy joy buzzer, also known as

10   an electro-shock-a-meter! Hides in the palm of your

11   hand. Pretty nifty, huh?

12 ROBIN: That hurt.

13 PAT: No, it just jolted your sensibilities a little. Kinda like

14   my outfit.

15 ROBIN: Well, I have to admit, I really wasn't expecting my

16   date to show up dressed as a frog.

17 PAT: It does get a good reaction.

18 ROBIN: Yeah, all my neighbors are staring. *(PAT turns around*

19   *and waves to all the neighbors.)*

20 PAT: Oh. Hi, everybody.

21 ROBIN: Do you like shocking people?

22 PAT: Apparently, I do. It seems to be a reoccurring theme

23   in my life.

24 ROBIN: And how long has this been a reoccurring theme in

25   your life?

1   PAT: Two years. Ever since I got struck by lightning.
2   ROBIN: Wow, I didn't know about that. What was that like?
3   PAT: Big, hot, and bright, *and really shocking!*
4   ROBIN: Wow. Hold on. *(Calling off)* Dad! I found somebody to
5   jump-start the car!

Shy

Introduction

In this scene, "shy is the word" as two country bumpkins try their hand at courting.

1   PAT: I really like you, **Robin.** *(Chuckles shyly.)*

2   ROBIN: I like you, too, **Pat.** *(Shy little laugh)* **Tee-hee.**

3   PAT: You're so pretty. *(Shyly)* **Uhhhh-huhhhh.**

4   ROBIN: You're so **handsome.** *(Followed by a high-pitched*

5   *sigh)*

6   PAT: Will you be my girlfriend? *(PAT turns away. Under his*

7   *breath)* **Oh-boy, oh-boy, oh-boy.**

8   ROBIN: Yes, if you want me to. *(ROBIN flutters her eyelids and*

9   *turns away shyly. PAT turns back to her.)*

10 PAT: So — uh — so — uh — can I give you a kiss? *(ROBIN*

11   *turns back to him.)*

12 ROBIN: **Uh-huh.** *(ROBIN closes her eyes and puckers up,*

13   *waiting for the big moment. PAT closes his eyes, puckers up,*

14   *and leans in, but then he misses her face completely. They*

15   *end up bumping shoulders and both open their eyes and*

16   *giggle shyly. They then close their eyes, pucker up, lean in,*

17   *and miss again. They both open their eyes and giggle shyly.)*

18 PAT: **This is harder than I thought it would be.**

19 ROBIN: **It sure is. Big sister and her beau don't seem to**

20   **have this much trouble.**

21 PAT: **It sure wasn't this hard when I was practicing.**

22 ROBIN: *(Shocked)* **You been practicing?** *With who?*

23 PAT: **With that old knothole in Grandma's peach tree. I**

24   **pretended it was you and I kissed it a couple of times.**

25 ROBIN: **Oh, that's so sweet.** *(And with that, ROBIN hauls off*

1   *and kisses PAT smack on the lips for a long time. When they*
2   *break, they both turn away from each other and giggle —*
3   *shyly.)*

Silly

Introduction

"If there's a speck in your brother's eye — " Oh, well! Obviously, ROBIN's never heard of that scripture.

1 *(As the scene opens, PAT is parading in a circle around his*
2 *sister making turkey noises.)*
3 **ROBIN: What are you doing?**
4 **PAT:** *(Makes turkey noises.)* **I'm a turkey.**
5 **ROBIN: You certainly are. Why are you being so silly?**
6 **PAT: Because** *(Turkey noises)* **it's fun.**
7 **ROBIN: No, it's silly and it's stupid.**
8 **PAT: Says who? Besides, I don't care. At least I'm not stuck**
9 **up.**
10 **ROBIN: What? What are you saying? Are you calling me**
11 *stuck up?*
12 **PAT: If the shoe fits.** *(Turkey noises)*
13 **ROBIN: You turkey. I'm not stuck up. I'm refined!**
14 **PAT: No, you're a stuck up. A card-carrying, nose-in-the-air,**
15 **FDA-certified stuck up!** *(Turkey noises)*
16 **ROBIN: Oh, no, I'm not.**
17 **PAT: Yes, you are! You are, you are.**
18 **ROBIN: Humphf! And how do you know, huh? Prove it.**
19 **PAT: OK. Lean your head back and stick your nose way up**
20 **in the air.** *(ROBIN does so.)*
21 **ROBIN: OK. Now what?**
22 **PAT: Now, see if you can drop your chin back down to your**
23 **chest. You can't, can you?** *(ROBIN tries, but can't put her*
24 *head down. Her nose is stuck up high in the air.)*
25 **ROBIN: Ahhhh! Mom! Help! I can't put my head down!**

1   *(ROBIN runs off the stage in a panic. PAT follows her, making*
2   *like he is flapping his wings.)*
3   **PAT: Told ya!** *(Turkey noises)*

Simple

Introduction
In this scene, two parents try to figure out a way to tell their Down syndrome son that his sister has died in a freak accident.

1 ROBIN: Tommy's not really going to understand any of this,
2   do you think?
3 PAT: I don't know. He may. In his own simple way. We won't
4   know until we talk to him.
5 ROBIN: I mean, I think Tommy'll get the fact that his little
6   sister isn't here right now, but do you think he'll
7   understand anything else?
8 PAT: I don't know. Just because he's got Down syndrome
9   ... He understands a lot more than you think sometimes.
10 ROBIN: You think? He's so simple in so many ways.
11 PAT: Then we'll have to keep this simple, too.
12 ROBIN: Yeah. I guess.
13 PAT: It's hard to realize we're never going to see her again
14   ... in this lifetime. *(Thinking what to do, they sit in silence*
15   *for a long moment.)*
16 ROBIN: Just because he's simple doesn't mean his love for
17   his little sister isn't deep. He adores her. *(A moment of*
18   *silence as ROBIN looks up at PAT and searches his face with*
19   *her eyes.)* Is "did" the right word now? *(ROBIN breaks out*
20   *in sobs and buries her face into PAT's shoulder. He holds her.)*
21 PAT: Shhhh. I love you.
22 ROBIN: How is he going to fill the hole in his heart?
23 PAT: How will any of us?
24 ROBIN: I miss her already.
25 PAT: Me too.

1   ROBIN: "Keep it simple," you said. I never knew anything so
2   simple could be so hard.

Sympathetic

Introduction
In this scene, an inconsiderate girl gets a lesson about the Golden Rule from her slightly jaded TEDDY BEAR.

1 GIRL: Oh, Teddy Bear, my arm hurts so bad.

2 TEDDY BEAR: Sorry, kid, what can I say?

3 GIRL: Teddy, you talked! I can't believe this.

4 TEDDY BEAR: Surprise, surprise, surprise! Aren't we all full
5   of surprises?

6 GIRL: But — why have you never talked before?

7 TEDDY BEAR: Well, actually, I'm not supposed to. It's
8   against the rules, you know — it's contractual and
9   there's all this legal mumbo jumbo.

10 GIRL: But you're talking now!

11 TEDDY BEAR: Yeah, I know. Look, frankly, I, uh, just
12   couldn't hold back any longer, I guess. I mean, I'm
13   supposed to be sorry you broke your arm and all —
14   that's my job — but actually I'm not really feeling all
15   that sympathetic about it.

16 GIRL: But why not? You're my teddy.

17 TEDDY BEAR: I know. I know. It's just that you were pretty
18   ... what's the right word ... *lackadaisical* — yeah, that's
19   it — *lackadaisical* when Bowzer got a hold of me last
20   week and chewed half of *my* arm off! I mean, *(Mimicking*
21   *her response to his tragedy)* "Oh, well! He's just a doll!"
22   *(Sarcastically)* Thanks a lot for nothin'!

23 GIRL: But Teddy, I didn't know you were alive then!

24 TEDDY BEAR: No?

25 GIRL: No!

1   TEDDY BEAR: So? What difference does it make? Baby girl,
2   I'm your Teddy Bear. Nobody loves you as much as I do.
3   GIRL: But I didn't know! I'm sorry. I should have taken
4   better care of you. Come here and let me hold you. I'll
5   make it up to you. I promise. *(TEDDY BEAR goes to her.*
6   *GIRL squeezes him tight. He pulls away.)*
7   TEDDY BEAR: Hey, hey! Watch the arm, OK?

Teasing

Introduction
In this scene, we find out that one good turn deserves another with brothers and sisters.

1 PAT: Robin has a boyfriend! Robin has a boyfriend!

2 ROBIN: Shut up, Pat! I do not.

3 PAT: I saw you kissing Tommy on the porch.

4 ROBIN: And I'm going to kill you with a torch!

5 PAT: What? Now we're speaking in rhymes?

6 ROBIN: Only if it will get you to shut up.

7 PAT: Well, I don't know. I kinda like your boyfriend.

8 ROBIN: I tell you, Tommy's not my boyfriend.

9 PAT: Then, why did you let him kiss you?

10 ROBIN: I don't know. I just did.

11 PAT: You kissed a boy! You kissed a boy!

12 ROBIN: So what? You can't hold your tobacco! You can't

13   hold your tobacco!

14 PAT: What?

15 ROBIN: Harold told me — the other night at the rodeo — he

16   gave you a chaw of Redman and in five minutes you

17   turned greener than a Granny apple!

18 PAT: Did not.

19 ROBIN: Puked all over your new boots.

20 PAT: They — they didn't tell me how to do it right.

21 ROBIN: You threw up! You threw up!

22 PAT: Shhhh! Not so loud. Mom and Dad would kill me if

23   they knew.

24 ROBIN: So, we through teasing each other? Never going to

25   discuss either one of these again?

1   PAT: Yeah, I guess so.
2   ROBIN: Good, 'cause I gotta go get ready for my date
3   tonight with Tommy.

Tense

Introduction
There are lots of different types of "tenses"!

1   *(As the scene opens, we find ROBIN giving her boyfriend,*
2   *PAT, a back rub.)*
3   ROBIN: Oh, your muscles are so tense!
4   PAT: I know. You've found every knot in my back.
5   ROBIN: I've never seen your back so tight before. What
6   happened?
7   PAT: I got all tense in English class today. First, there were
8   the nouns and then the adjectives.
9   ROBIN: And then — the verbs?
10   PAT: Yep, you guessed it: tenses! Present tense, past tense,
11   passive tense, gerunds, participles. All of them.
12   ROBIN: Yikes!
13   PAT: Past perfect tense. It was a beating!
14   ROBIN: You poor thing. No wonder you're so ... *you know!*
15   So, how are your arms? Your hands?
16   PAT: Knotted. Knotted. Tight and swollen.
17   ROBIN: Well, at least now you're finished with that.
18   PAT: Yeah, with the verbs! Now comes the adverbs!
19   ROBIN: Oh, dear.
20   PAT: Just thinking about it makes me really hurt.
21   ROBIN: Where? Are you sore here?
22   PAT: Very.
23   ROBIN: Now? How should I rub it? Quickly or slowly?
24   PAT: Briskly. And deeply, too.
25   ROBIN: *(She rubs him for a little while.)* I can't do this much

1   more. I'm getting pretty tired. Is this enough already?

2 PAT: Never, never, never.

Trouble

Introduction

In this scene, ROBIN, a Disney World employee, is escorting PAT, an unruly guest, out of the park.

1   ROBIN: Here's the exit, sir. Good-bye.

2   PAT: I really don't want to go. I love Disney World!

3   ROBIN: Yes, but Disney World does not love you. You caused

4   us a lot of trouble today.

5   PAT: I made a mistake.

6   ROBIN: You were fishing in the *mermaid tank!*

7   PAT: I know. I'm sorry. But, can you blame me? They really

8   do put up a fight! It was pretty thrilling while it lasted.

9   ROBIN: Sir, those were not fish! They were girls in mermaid

10   suits!

11   PAT: She swam all over that tank.

12   ROBIN: She almost drowned because of you.

13   PAT: I'd pull back, and then I'd lean in, reel her in a little. It

14   was fun! And then I pulled really hard and up came the

15   prettiest fish you ever saw.

16   ROBIN: Sir, she was not a fish! *She was a girl!*

17   PAT: *No! Worse!* She was my sister-in-law.

18   ROBIN: *(Surprised)* Jeanie's your sister-in-law?

19   PAT: Yep, and she's going to kill me. And then, my brother's

20   going to kill me. I thought she worked at the mermaid

21   gift shop. I didn't know she ... Couldn't I just hide out

22   here for a couple of weeks until this thing kind of blows

23   over? Say ... out in the Wilderness Trailer Park?

24   ROBIN: Nope.

25   PAT: Please? Pretty please with sugar on top!

1 ROBIN: No way, Jose.
2 PAT: I promise I'll be good. No more fishing. I'll work as
3   Mickey Mouse for free.
4 ROBIN: Absolutely not. We have our standards.
5 PAT: Great. Just send me off to my doom.

Males Only

Scenes are written for two males

Ability

Introduction

Sometimes, the history books get it wrong! Witness now what really happened the day ARTHUR pulled Excalibur out of the stone and became King of England. It all started when he and LANCELOT, two teenagers, were messing around and ...

1   LANCELOT: I can't believe it. You just pulled the stinking
2   sword out of the stone! How'd you do that?
3   ARTHUR: I don't know. I just grabbed the handle and
4   pulled.
5   LANCELOT: Nobody's ever done that before!
6   ARTHUR: I know. But *I* just did!
7   LANCELOT: They say Merlin put it there! And only the real
8   heir to the crown can pull it out.
9   ARTHUR: So, what does this mean? Am I going to be king?
10 LANCELOT: *(Incredulous)* Yeah, whatever! Dude, hurry up
11   and put it back before somebody sees us and we're in
12   trouble.
13 ARTHUR: Why? Maybe I don't want to put it back. Maybe I
14   want to be king.
15 LANCELOT: But why? All it is is a bunch of headaches and
16   parading around waving at people.
17 ARTHUR: Well, somebody's got to do it? Why not me?
18 LANCELOT: Because! A king has to be strong and brave ...
19   and a leader.
20 ARTHUR: I'm strong. Been working out! Up to one-twenty-
21   five now bench pressing!
22 LANCELOT: I know. But is being number one in the
23   "Weakling Class" enough?
24 ARTHUR: And I'm brave. Picked up a dead mouse for Mum
25   in the kitchen the other night! Carried it right out and

1   tossed the nasty thing to the cat.

2 LANCELOT: My gosh! You may be the *one*. But are you a

3   leader?

4 ARTHUR: Of course I am. *(In a royal voice)* **Kneel subject,**

5   **and I will knight you.**

6 LANCELOT: And what if I don't want to?

7 ARTHUR: *(Still in the royal voice)* **Then I'll whack off your**

8   **head with Excalibur, you silly surf!** *(LANCELOT kneels and*

9   *ARTHUR taps him on both shoulders with the sword.)*

10 LANCELOT: Cool! And the knights get the girls, right?

Apathetic

Introduction

In this scene, Dr. FRANKENSTEIN finds out just how far apathy will get you when you ignore the needs of your laboratory help — mainly, IGOR!

1 IGOR: Master! Master! Master! The monster bit me. Help!
2   It's an emergency!
3 FRANKENSTEIN: Not now, Igor! Can't you see that I'm
4   busy?
5 IGOR: But, my hand!
6 FRANKENSTEIN: Oh, puff and nonsense. Be a man. Shake
7   it off!
8 IGOR: I'm bleeding to death!
9 FRANKENSTEIN: Of course you are. We all are. We're all
10   suffering for science! Go on and get yourself some
11   Neosporin and a Band-Aid. They're in the medicine
12   cabinet.
13 IGOR: But — but — that's not going to be enough. I need
14   stitches! Please! I beg you!
15 FRANKENSTEIN: Igor, I hate to tell you this, but you have
16   a long history of overreacting!
17 IGOR: You mean, like how I cried that time you splashed
18   sulfuric acid on my face?
19 FRANKENSTEIN: Yes. You complain about everything!
20 IGOR: Or like how I laid on the floor and whimpered after
21   you dropped that hundred-pound weight on my foot?
22 FRANKENSTEIN: Now you're getting the picture.
23 IGOR: Or how I screamed like a banshee after you made me
24   breathe that toxic gas?
25 FRANKENSTEIN: Exactly! And where would we be now if I'd

1   stopped my work to attend to you and all your little
2   complaints? Hmmmm? Absolutely nowhere! No
3   progress, no discoveries, no scientific breakthroughs, no
4   nothing! So, from now on, let's all just try to keep a
5   *good stiff upper lip,* shall we? *(A beat)* All right? Let's go
6   back to work. Hand me that liquid nitrogen, but be
7   careful! Spray it on anything and it'll be instantly frozen
8   in place! *(IGOR gets the bottle and immediately sprays*
9   *FRANKENSTEIN in the face.)*
10 IGOR: Do you mean like this?
11 FRANKENSTEIN: Awwww! *(Garbled speech)* Ooooh! My
12   upper lip! It's frozen! *(Covering his mouth, FRANKENSTEIN*
13   *flees the stage in agony.)*
14 IGOR: *(Calling after)* Hold on, boss! I'll get the Neosporin!

Bickering

Introduction
We all know that brothers sometimes fight, but occasionally, as we find out in this scene, they do it for a good reason.

1 HAROLD: You mean to tell me you're so hard up you had to
2   knock some poor kid off his bike, steal it, and then pawn
3   it off just so you'll have money to take your stupid
4   girlfriend out?
5 KIP: Yeah. For Peggy.
6 HAROLD: You're a creep, you know that?
7 KIP: Look who's talking!
8 HAROLD: For crying out loud, he was just a little kid!
9   You've probably traumatized him.
10 KIP: Well, I'm sorry about that, but I needed the bike.
11 HAROLD: To pawn?
12 KIP: What else could I do?
13 HAROLD: Getting your head examined comes to mind.
14 KIP: Get off my back.
15 HAROLD: Get off mine.
16 KIP: I'm not on yours.
17 HAROLD: No, but the police are! And when they get here
18   and want me to point out the bike thief, I'm going to
19   turn around and point at you, and they're going to haul
20   your worthless carcass off to jail!
21 KIP: You wouldn't dare.
22 HAROLD: Oh, no? You just watch me. I'm not covering for
23   you anymore.
24 KIP: You are one sorry excuse for a brother.
25 HAROLD: Now look who's talking.

1   **KIP: Moron!**

2   **HAROLD: Idiot!** *(The sound of the door bell. They look at the*

3   *door and then look at each other and freeze.)*

Bold

Introduction

In this scene, BLACKY, the famous pirate, addresses his men. One crewmember, ARRRR, is especially attentive.

1   BLACKY: I needs me men on this voyage who are ruthless
2   and who'll laugh in the face of danger! Men who can trim
3   the sail with one hand and swing a broadsword with
4   t'other!
5   ARRRR: Aye, Captain, that we are! We can do it! We're the
6   crew you want!
7   BLACKY: You there. You seem most enthusiastic. What's
8   your name?
9   ARRRR: Arrrr, sir!
10 BLACKY: Arrrr? A most unusual moniker for a sailor.
11 ARRRR: Aye, Captain, it is, but I was born on the seven
12   seas and never left her. My mammy and pappy saw the
13   sea water in me veins and brought me up on a diet of
14   tuna and squid.
15 BLACKY: A right hardy fella, are ya?
16 ARRRR: Aye, I am, sir. The sea is me home and danger is
17   what I live fer!
18 BLACKY: Danger? Just how bold are ye, eh? Are ye willing
19   to risk life and limb?
20 ARRRR: Aye, sir. Without blinkin' an eye.
21 BLACKY: *(Rising in enthusiasm)* Are ye bold enough to face
22   British cannons? Bold enough to beguile mermaids, yet
23   wiley enough to escape their murderous seduction? Bold
24   enough to live all your days with a bounty on your head
25   — willing to risk swinging at the end of a gallow's rope?

1   **ARRRR:** *(Equally enthusiastic)* **More than willing, Captain!**
2   **I've dreamt of it me whole life!**
3   **BLACKY: Then, you're me man! Good for you! Now for the**
4   **first order of business: Somebody's gotta clean the head**
5   *(The toilet)*! **It's really ...** *nasty!* **How about** *you?* *(BLACKY*
6   *leans towards ARRRR and smirks. ARRRR manages a weak*
7   *smile before suddenly jumping to the side and pointing off at*
8   *something in the distance. BLACKY looks, too.)*
9   **ARRRR: Oh, look Captain!** *It's the whole British fleet!*
10 **BLACKY: Well, shiver me timbers if it ain't!**
11 **ARRR:** *(Relieved)* **Yep, sure is. Guess our number's up. Well,**
12   **see ya on the gallows, Boss!** *(ARRRR exits off.)*
13 **BLACKY:** *(Disgusted)* **What some people won't do to get out**
14   **of a little work!**

Brave

Introduction

Being a soldier is often a thankless and dangerous job. In this scene, we honor the bravery of two American Marines, JOE and BOB, who are in an intense firefight.

1   JOE: They've got Johnson pinned down and he's hit.

2   BOB: I know. I know.

3   JOE: Well, what are we going to do? He won't last without
4   any help.

5   BOB: You're the sergeant. You tell me.

6   JOE: Well, somebody's got to go out there and get to him.

7   BOB: Is that an order or are you just talking out loud?

8   JOE: No. No, it's not an order.

9   BOB: So, what are we going to do?

10   JOE: We have to make a move. Check your gun.

11   BOB: Yes, sir. Don't you think we ought to wait for
12   reinforcements, sir?

13   JOE: I don't think Johnson can last that long. You ready?

14   BOB: Yes, sir.

15   JOE: OK, give me cover. I'm going to lob a couple of
16   grenades their direction and hopefully that will keep
17   them down. Then I can get to Johnson.

18   BOB: That's a pretty brave thing to do, sir.

19   JOE: Well, that's what we're made for. We're Marines.

20   BOB: Yes, sir. I'll give you good cover, sir. I'll keep 'em
21   down.

22   JOE: I know you will. Ready to go?

23   BOB: Yes, sir! You say when and I've got you covered.

24   JOE: One — two — three — *now! (BOB stands and starts*
25   *shooting. JOE stands and runs Off-Stage.)*

121

Chilling Out

Introduction
We all need to learn not to jump to conclusions just as LOU and STU, two cool video-game-playing dudes aptly demonstrate.

1   LOU: Hey man, you got the Coke?

2   STU: You know it, dude.

3   LOU: Well, where is it?

4   STU: It's in my car.

5   LOU: You left it in your car? You idiot. The heat will trash it,

6   dude.

7   STU: Nah, it's not going to hurt it.

8   LOU: Not hurt you maybe. Let's go get it.

9   STU: Can't. My parents are gone in the car.

10 LOU: You left the Coke out, man, where your parents could

11   find it?

12 STU: Yeah, it's no big thing. They dig it, too.

13 LOU: You're kidding? I thought they'd be all into beer and

14   wine.

15 STU: Nah. They like Coke.

16 LOU: Dude, that's awesome. My folks don't do Coke at all.

17 STU: Well, you should turn them onto it.

18 LOU: Yeah. Yeah, maybe I should.

19 STU: Hey, I think I just heard the car drive up.

20 LOU: We gonna be able to get the Coke anytime soon, you

21   think?

22 STU: Sure. As soon as they're in the house. We'll go get it.

23 LOU: You got any ice? If those Cokes have been in the car

24   all day, they're going to be hot and I hate drinking hot

25   pop.

1   STU: Yeah, me too. In the freezer: ice cream! I think I'm
2   gonna have a float. You wanna float?
3   LOU: Oh, dude, that sounds awesome.

Consequences

Introduction

Sometimes we don't find trouble, trouble finds us. This scene takes place in the family car after DAD has just bailed SON out of jail.

1 DAD: I don't know what to say. The only thing I can think
2   of is: Why did you do it?
3 SON: I don't know.
4 DAD: *"I don't know"* is not an answer, Junior! I just had to
5   bail my only son out of jail because he just participated
6   in an armed robbery! I need an answer!
7 SON: Dad, I didn't do anything. I was just in the car!
8 DAD: It makes no difference. *It makes no difference!* In the
9   eyes of the law, you're just as guilty as that thug,
10   Maleak, with the gun.
11 SON: I didn't know, Dad. I didn't know. OK? I'm sorry. I
12   goofed.
13 DAD: That's an understatement! Do you know how much
14   trouble you're in? You're sixteen-years-old and charged
15   with armed robbery! Do you know they can certify you as
16   an adult? You may go away to prison — and I'm not
17   talking juvie — I'm talking big-time, grown-up, adult
18   prison! And *I know* you don't want to go there!
19 SON: I know, Dad, I know.
20 DAD: No, you don't! *No,* you don't. *And your momma!?*
21   Whadya gonna tell her, huh? And your scholarship
22   chances? Poof! You can kiss them good-bye. I can just
23   about guarantee you that. And your car? Bye-bye. It cost
24   a lot of money to get a lawyer.
25 SON: *OK, Dad! I get it! I get it! OK?* How many times do I

1   have to say it?
2 DAD: As many times as it takes for you to explain to me
3   how you got mixed up in this!
4 SON: I don't know ... I just wanted to fit in ... I didn't know
5   nothin' like that was going to happen. Honest. We was
6   just cruising around when Deirre all of a sudden pulled
7   into this parking lot and Maleak jumped out! And before
8   I knew it, he was back in the car and everybody was
9   screaming and hollering and we were speeding away,
10   and then the next thing I knew, there was cop cars and
11   sirens and they had guns pointed at us. *(Begins to cry.)*
12   And it was scary, Dad, so scary. I thought I was gonna
13   die! *(SON sobs. After a moment, DAD reaches over and*
14   *squeezes SON on the shoulder.)*
15 DAD: OK. We're going to get through this, OK? Whatever it
16   takes. We'll get through it.

Dependable

Introduction

Holy cow, crime fighters, not all is well in the secret lair of FATMAN.

1   *(As the scene opens, FATMAN is giving BOBIN a quiz while*
2   *BOBIN is busy doing jumping jacks.)*
3   FATMAN: So, Bobin, when you take the Fatmobile to
4   Starbucks, what kind of latte do I like?
5   BOBIN: Caramel mocha cream with a touch of hazelnuts
6   and chocolate sprinkles.
7   FATMAN: Correct! And when you stop by the news stand,
8   what newspapers do you get?
9   BOBIN: *USA Today, New York Times,* and *Frotham Planet.*
10 FATMAN: Absolutely! And when picking up breakfast?
11 BOBIN: IHOP's Rooty Tooty Fresh 'N Fruity.
12 FATMAN: Good job! And what's the most important
13   characteristic of a superhero sidekick?
14 BOBIN: Dependability?
15 FATMAN: Fantastic! Good job. You can stop now. *(BOBIN*
16   *stops. He's out of breath.)*
17 BOBIN: Holy cow, Fatman, I thought dependability was
18   more about knowing what your partner's going to do at
19   any given moment of a high-stress situation. Like that
20   time we were fighting the Jester and you passed him off
21   to me so you could go rescue Ricki Rale. I knew exactly
22   what you were doing and when you were going to do it.
23   So, when you spun him around to face me, I was ready
24   and I really let him have it. *Wham! Ker-pow!*
25 FATMAN: That's true. That kind of dependability is the

1   foundation of all crime fighting.

2   BOBIN: So, why aren't we practicing *those* kinds of skills

3   instead of this other drivel?

4   FATMAN: Well, to be quite frank, Bobin, we've pretty well

5   cleaned up Frotham City. All the bad guys are locked

6   up. And as far as your crime fighting skills — I mean,

7   timing? Speed? Coordination? Phft! You've got it all. Kid,

8   you're the most dependable sidekick I've ever had.

9   BOBIN: Whoa, wait a minute. What do you mean "ever

10   had"? Does that mean you've *had* other sidekicks? Is

11   that what you're saying? So, what happened to those

12   other guys?

13   FATMAN: *(Fumbling)* What? Uh — no, not at all! Just you,

14   Junior Crime Fighter! Just you! *(FATMAN hurriedly exits.*

15   *A suspicious BOBIN watches him go.)*

16   BOBIN: Hmmmm? Maybe, from here on out, I *ought not be*

17   so dependable!

Disgusting

Introduction

In this scene, we find out that everybody has their limits — even the hired help.

1 (As the scene opens, JEEVES, the butler, watches over Sir
2 WILSON as he finishes his dinner.)
3 WILSON: Jeeves, I'm not happy. The pot roast was
4   undercooked, and the silverware's spotty.
5 JEEVES: My apologies, sir. I will reprimand the cook. It will
6   not happen again.
7 WILSON: Well, it had better not!
8 JEEVES: Very good, sir. Is there anything else I can do?
9 WILSON: Yes, Jeeves, there is! I somehow managed to drop
10   my napkin on the floor a while ago, would you be so kind
11   as to pick it up for me?
12 JEEVES: My pleasure, sir. (JEEVES bends over to pick up the
13   napkin. As he does, there is a loud ripping sound. WILSON
14   gasps. Realizing that the back of his pants have ripped,
15   JEEVES straightens back up with as much dignity as he
16   can.)
17 WILSON: Oh, Jeeves! Tut-tut-tut-tut-tut. I can't tell you how
18   disgusting that was.
19 JEEVES: Yes, sir. Sorry, sir. I fear I had no idea the pants
20   were — I am so embarrassed.
21 WILSON: As well you should be! If there's one thing I
22   demand in this house, it's decorum!
23 JEEVES: Yes, sir. Decorum. I understand, sir. May I be
24   released to change now, sir?
25 WILSON: Released? No, you're not "released." You're fired!

1   Go on. I have no use for a slovenly, unprofessional twit
2   like you! Off with you!
3   JEEVES: But, sir! My pants. Please, I implore you, let me
4   change first. Think of my position. Please don't let the
5   rest of the staff see me this way. Allow me to preserve
6   my dignity.
7   WILSON: Dignity-gigady! Poof! Bah! Go. Out the front door
8   with you! Now!
9   JEEVES: Very well, then. If you insist. *(With military precision*
10 *and great dignity, JEEVES goes to exit, but before he leaves,*
11 *he stops and turns back around.)* Oh! One thing more, sir.
12 Before I go.
13 WILSON: Yes, yes, what is it? Make it quick. *(JEEVES sticks*
14 *out his tongue and gives WILSON a raspberry, then exits with*
15 *full honor.)*

Hesitating

Introduction

Making progress is never easy. In this scene, we step back in time to Ancient Rome and find a fashion model and his designer discussing the latest innovations in clothing.

1 NERO: Oh, Cleo, you are just the cat's meow when it comes
2   to designs.
3 CLEO: Thanks, Nero, but you know, I couldn't have done it
4   without you. You make all my stuff look great on the
5   runway.
6 NERO: But I gotta tell ya. This outfit *really* makes me
7   uncomfortable.
8 CLEO: Really? But *why?*
9 NERO: I don't know. I'm afraid it's just too — too over the
10   top.
11 CLEO: Nero, what are you talking about? Dude, you're my
12   best model. *You* sell my designs! For the last six
13   seasons. People are going to see you in this and it'll be
14   flying off the rack!
15 NERO: I don't know about this one, Cleo.
16 CLEO: Trust me. People are going to love this outfit. And
17   this time next week, everybody who's anybody in Rome
18   will either be wearing one or wanting one.
19 NERO: Do you really think so?
20 CLEO: I know so. This is going to change history!
21 NERO: But look at it! The idea is just so ludicrous: You've
22   sewn two tubes together and joined them in the middle.
23   And you're supposed to pull them up your legs and tie
24   a rope around your waist? And what did you call them?
25   *Pants!* And these are for men?

1 CLEO: Mmmm-hmmmm. I know. Yep. They're going to be
2   the next big thing. Exciting, isn't it?
3 NERO: But they're going to show off the shape of my legs
4   — and my rear!
5 CLEO: Don't worry, your tunic will cover it up!
6 NERO: But what if, Cleo? What if they *don't* catch on? Don't
7   sell?
8 CLEO: Oh, but they will.
9 NERO: But, what if they don't? What are we going to do
10   then?
11 CLEO: Well, if that happens, I'll just take them all back, cut
12   'em up, and use them on my next project! It's going to
13   be kinda like a tunic, but it's going to have arm
14   coverings attached. I think I'll call it "a coat." So, if they
15   don't work on the legs, we'll make 'em work on the
16   arms!

Hungry

Introduction

In this scene, Yellowstone National Park's Ranger RICK is in the midst of interrogating camper CARL after a horrendous incident in the park.

1   RICK: Gee, I don't know. I'm pretty sure something illegal's
2   happened here.
3   CARL: I'm so sorry, Mr. Ranger, sir. I didn't — It's just that
4   ... I've been lost for three days now, and I haven't had
5   anything to eat, and I'd just wandered into this clearing
6   and was glancing around and thinking about that old
7   sayin', you know, *(Best mountain man's voice)* "I'm so
8   hungry I could eat a bear," *(Back to normal voice)* when
9   he walked out of the woods! And I looked at him and he
10   looked at me and well ... one thing just kinda led to
11   another.
12 RICK: But a *grizzly? You ate a grizzly!* They're huge! How is
13   this humanly possible? This is beyond comprehension.
14 CARL: If it wasn't for the hair in my teeth, and this awful
15   aftertaste, I wouldn't believe it either. Yuck.
16 RICK: And you say you just ate him whole? Didn't he fight
17   you? Bite you? Claw you?
18 CARL: Apparently he got me a little on this arm, but it all
19   went down pretty fast. I was awfully hungry. *(A beat)* Oh,
20   wow, I think I'm getting sick.
21 RICK: You do know, regardless how you killed it, they are
22   protected animals. They're an endangered species.
23 CARL: I know, I know. I figured there's going to be some
24   kind of fine to pay or something.
25 RICK: A fine? *Fines nothing!* We're talking prison time here,

1   mister. Heck, I'm not sure I don't need to call Homeland
2   Security!
3 CARL: Homeland Security? Why?
4 RICK: *Because!* How many people do you know who go
5   around eating grizzly bears? Whole! Raw! Mister, you're
6   a threat to national security!
7 CARL: Well, normally not. Normally, I'm just an accountant
8   from little ol' Kemp, Texas.
9 RICK: Regardless, you sit down right there and just wait.
10   I've got to call headquarters. *(Speaking into cell phone)*
11   Hello? Boss? This is Rick. I'm out in section eighteen
12   and I have a ninety-nine-forty-one. *(Listens to the phone,*
13   *then speaks again.)* Yes, sir. That's what I said: a ninety-
14   nine-forty-one. *(Listens, then speaks.)* Boss? Boss? *(To*
15   *CARL)* I think he passed out.
16 CARL: I don't blame him. I think I am, too. Oh, I wish hadn't
17   eaten that last leg!

Introverted

Introduction

We all know that things don't always necessarily go as planned. But sometimes, interviewing a *shy* person can definitely be a *real* challenge.

1   REPORTER: Thank you for granting us this interview, sir,
2   and being on our TV show today. First off, let me
3   congratulate you on your new movie, *I Was There.* It's
4   getting great reviews.
5   RICHARD: Yes.
6   REPORTER: So, was this an exciting film to work on?
7   RICHARD: Oh, yes.
8   REPORTER: You had quite an interesting scene in the movie
9   with Cheryl Laine. Would you like to tell us about it?
10 RICHARD: No.
11 REPORTER: Would you care to summarize the plot for our
12   TV audience?
13 RICHARD: Not really.
14 REPORTER: You don't really like to talk much, do you? Well,
15   they say a lot of extroverted actors are really very
16   introverted people. Would that best describe you, sir?
17   *(REPORTER waits for an answer, but RICHARD just shrugs*
18   *his shoulders. REPORTER refers back to his notes for his next*
19   *question.)* OK. *(A beat)* Did you know that most film
20   critics hail you as a comic genius?
21 RICHARD: Yes, yes. I know that. Yes. That's true.
22 REPORTER: But I suspect you're not going to discuss your
23   creative process with us here today, are you? *(There is*
24   *only silence as RICHARD simply looks at REPORTER and*
25   *smiles.)* You really are shy, aren't you? You're staring

1   down at your shoes.

2   RICHARD: Yes, they're dirty. I stepped in some mud coming

3   in. *(A beat)* **Did you know there's ten different types of**

4   **soil within a fifty-mile radius of this place?**

5   REPORTER: No. Really? I didn't know that. Is that true?

6   RICHARD: No.

7   REPORTER: Right. Why am I not surprised?

Irritating

Introduction
This scene is inspired by the comic duo of Laurel and Hardy.

1   *(As this scene begins, we find STAN watching OLIVER busily*
2   *scratching himself.)*
3   **STAN: What are you doing, Ollie?**
4   **OLIVER: What am I — ? What does it look like I'm doing,**
5   **Stanley?**
6   **STAN: It looks like you're scratching.**
7   **OLIVER: That's right. That's what I'm doing. I got up this**
8   **morning and got dressed and now I'm itching all over.**
9   **So help me. Scratch my back!** *(STAN starts scratching*
10   *OLIVER's back.)* **No, over here, over here.**
11 **STAN: Here?**
12 **OLIVER: Yes, yes. Ooooh, yes.**
13 **STAN: Feelin' better?**
14 **OLIVER: A little, but — oh — but now my arms are itching!**
15   *(OLIVER starts scratching his arms. Then, he starts scratching*
16   *his legs. STAN all the while is scratching his back. As the*
17   *scene proceeds, OLIVER is wildly scratching everywhere.)*
18 **STAN: Stand still. Stop dancing so.**
19 **OLIVER: I can't help it. It's just getting worse. Over here!**
20   **Over here! Scratch harder!**
21 **STAN: You sure are irritable today.**
22 **OLIVER: You'd be irritable, too, if you were itching like me.**
23 **STAN: I think you have "irritable irritation" syndrome! You**
24   **should learn to relax better.**
25 **OLIVER: Oh, do be quiet, Stanley. Oh! I'm itchy all over! I**

1   wish I knew why this was happening.

2   STAN: Oh, I don't know, Ollie, maybe it was that bottle of

3   itching powder I split in your suitcase!

4   OLIVER: *You did what!?* Ooooh, you! *(OLIVER hits STAN with*

5   *his hat and then chases STAN off the stage.)*

Knowledgeable

Introduction
Knowledge sometimes comes from the most unexpected sources. In this scene, the PROFESSOR's lecture is suddenly interrupted by an enlightening stranger.

1 PROFESSOR: The crater ratio of the middle crust is a
2   modicum past nine point four.
3 BOB: You sure are knowledgeable about geophysics.
4 PROFESSOR: Thank you, young man. Do you have a
5   question?
6 BOB: Yes, sir, I do. How much do you know about Carla?
7 PROFESSOR: Excuse me? Carla?
8 BOB: Carla Diane Malloy? *Your daughter?*
9 PROFESSOR: *(Befuddled)* Carla? What do you mean "what
10   do I know about Carla?"
11 BOB: I mean: How knowledgeable are you of your own flesh
12   and blood? Know what her favorite color is? Food? Rock
13   group? TV show?
14 PROFESSOR: Right off the top of my head, no, I can't say
15   I do. But you've caught me off guard. Are you on my roll
16   sheet? Who exactly are you again?
17 BOB: Bob, Doc. Bob.
18 PROFESSOR: Well *Bob,* what exactly is your point?
19 BOB: My point is you seem to know so much about all these
20   *things,* but you seem to know so little about the one
21   person in the world you should know about.
22 PROFESSOR: Bob, I don't know you, but I don't like you. I
23   think I need to call security.
24 BOB: Did you know that her drug of choice is *cocaine?*
25 PROFESSOR: What? Excuse me!

138

1 BOB: Or that she's been slipping out of her bedroom
2   window every night for the past six weeks and going
3   clubbing with a twenty-three-year-old guy and then
4   slipping back in at four in the morning? I'd bet you
5   probably don't even know that she couldn't care less
6   about her grades and that she thinks you're a real loser.
7 PROFESSOR: And you'd be right. But I do now. And tell
8   me, *who* are you again, Bob?
9 BOB: Let's just say I'm a twenty-three-year-old guy who's
10   developed a "modicum" of a conscience.

Logical

Introduction

It seems that sometimes, even our favorite outer space dudes have off days, too. In this scene, we find Captain KOOK and Mr. SMOCK on the deck of the USS Centerprise.

1 SMOCK: Captain, that's totally illogical.

2 KOOK: Well, Smock, what would you suggest?

3 SMOCK: I would suggest the white dress with the small

4   green polka-dots.

5 KOOK: Even after Easter?

6 SMOCK: Yes, Captain.

7 KOOK: But you don't think the fit will be too tight? And the

8   pillbox hat?

9 SMOCK: A logical choice. I've seen many Rulcan females

10   sporting such hats.

11 KOOK: It's so hard to shop for a woman.

12 SMOCK: I'm afraid I have to agree with you on that one,

13   Captain.

14 KOOK: That's good, good. You agree with me so seldom,

15   Smock.

16 SMOCK: That's because, as a human, you're so emotional.

17 KOOK: Has there ever been a time when your logic hasn't

18   served you well?

19 SMOCK: Well, there was that one time.

20 KOOK: That one time?

21 SMOCK: I was needing to hurry back to the Centerprise and

22   I thought the logical thing to do was to take a taxi.

23 KOOK: And it wasn't?

24 SMOCK: No.

25 KOOK: Why?

1 SMOCK: Because all the tires were flat.

2 KOOK: Ahhhh.

3 SMOCK: I was so embarrassed.

4 KOOK: That's logical.

Nervous

Introduction

As we all know, we all need help sometimes. In this scene, PAT tries to help his nervous roommate get ready for his first date.

1 PAT: Man, you are so nervous. Look at you. You're shaking
2   like a leaf.
3 JOE: I know, but I can't help it. I've never been on a date
4   before.
5 PAT: You are just spending the evening with her. You're not
6   marrying the chick.
7 JOE: I know.
8 PAT: So, who are you going out with?
9 JOE: Shelby Boyd.
10 PAT: Shelby Boyd? *Shelby Boyd? The* Shelby Boyd is going
11   out with you?
12 JOE: Well ... yeah.
13 PAT: Dude, that is one major score. Shelby Boyd is going
14   out with a loser like you?
15 JOE: Hey, watch it! I'm not a loser, remember?
16 PAT: I've been trying to get a date with her for months.
17 JOE: Did you ask her?
18 PAT: Sure, I've asked her. Twenty different ways! I emailed
19   her. Texted her. Facebooked her. Even Twittered her.
20   And nothing! Not even a nibble! How'd you get her to go
21   out with you?
22 JOE: I stopped by her locker between classes and *asked*
23   her.
24 PAT: You *asked* her? You? Gee. Wow! What a novel idea.
25   You're braver than I thought.

1 JOE: Well, quit being such a loser, dude.

2 PAT: Just thinking about having to talk to her face to face

3 　　makes me nervous.

4 JOE: Me too.

5 PAT: But you already have.

6 JOE: All I did was walk up and say, "Will you go out with

7 　　me Saturday night?"

8 PAT: But now you gotta *really* talk to her. Involve her in "in-

9 　　tel-lect-ual" conversation.

10 JOE: I know. And that's what I'm really nervous about.

Pride

Introduction

We all know that sports are all about sportsmanship, right? Our scene picks up just after PAT and ROBIN have finished racing against each other.

1   PAT: Oh, that was a good race.

2   ROBIN: Yep, but I won.

3   PAT: Yes, you did. Good race. *(PAT offers his hand to ROBIN to*

4   *shake. ROBIN ignores it.)* Hey, that's not cool.

5   ROBIN: Deal with it, loser. Sportsmanship is so overrated.

6   I'm the one taking home the trophy today!

7   PAT: Well, take it. I'd rather be a good sport.

8   ROBIN: I will, and that is why you'll always lose and I'll

9   always win. Winning is everything.

10   PAT: Is that right?

11   ROBIN: Yep, and I have the drive and the desire. And the

12   self-pride.

13   PAT: Just remember, the Bible says "pride goes before a

14   fall."

15   ROBIN: *(Sarcastically)* Yeah, sure, right. I'm the winner

16   today! That's all there is to it.

17   PAT: Winner on the track. That's all.

18   ROBIN: What do you mean?

19   PAT: Nothing. You wouldn't understand.

20   ROBIN: No, wait. Go ahead. Explain yourself.

21   PAT: What would be the point? I got to meet my church

22   group. We're going to go take some Christmas gifts to

23   some orphans.

24   ROBIN: Orphans, huh? *(Snorts.)* Ha! Just another word for

25   losers, too! *(PAT waves ROBIN off and exits. ROBIN watches*

1   *him go and shakes his head as if to say, "What a loser!" He*
2   *then turns around, picks up his towel, and raises up and*
3   *starts to walk off, but trips and falls down. He immediately*
4   *pops back up. He glances around quickly, then exits. As he*
5   *goes)* **Gee, I hope nobody saw that.**

Reasoning

Introduction

In this scene, a wise old PREACHER has some sage advice for the new GROOM just before to the wedding starts.

1 PREACHER: Look, people do this every day. Thousands of
2   people. There's really nothing to be nervous about. You
3   just stand up there, hold her hand, look her in the eye,
4   and speak the truth.
5 GROOM: Speak? Oh, no! I can't. I can't! I'm no good at
6   this. I'm — I'm a stutterer!
7 PREACHER: Not before today.
8 GROOM: It came over me last night. Two a.m. I bolted up
9   and I realized deep in my soul that I was born with a
10   stutter.
11 PREACHER: You're not stuttering now.
12 GROOM: It — it — it — it comes and goes. I — I — won't
13   know what to say.
14 PREACHER: Just relax, I'm gonna tell you what to say.
15 GROOM: What — what — what if I don't really want to say
16   it? What if I've changed my mind? What if I want to call
17   the whole thing off?
18 PREACHER: Now, that's a whole different matter. But you
19   really don't want to do that, do you?
20 GROOM: I don't know.
21 PREACHER: No, no, you don't. You've just got the jitters.
22   You really do want to get up there and you really do want
23   to go through with this wedding ceremony, and I guess
24   deep down in your heart you know why.
25 GROOM: No. Why?

1   PREACHER: *(Building)* Because the bride — that little girl —
2   coming down the aisle in a thousand-dollar wedding
3   dress is *my daughter!* And if you think you're getting out
4   of this little production now, you are sorely mistaken!
5   Because if you don't follow me out there when we get the
6   signal, I'm going to knock your block off!
7   GROOM: *(Completely cowed)* Oh — oh — yes, sir. Whatever
8   you say, sir.
9   PREACHER: Good! And when we get out there, what are you
10   going to say?
11 GROOM: I do?

Resolve

Introduction
Wrong is wrong, right? In this scene, a lowly freshman, B-team player, seems to think so.

1　BILLY: Coach, you got a minute?

2　COACH: Quick. I got things to do. Whatdaya need, Jones?

3　BILLY: I needed to talk to you about practice yesterday. You
4　　embarrassed me. In front of everybody! You said I was
5　　slower than Christmas, that I had no talent, and that I
6　　was the worst player on the team.

7　COACH: Oh, that! I know you try. But you must know
8　　yourself you're not a very good player. It wasn't anything
9　　personal.

10　BILLY: But it was personal. You singled me out! I was
11　　embarrassed. I was humiliated!

12　COACH: Look, I was ... uh ... only trying to motivate people.
13　　Now, if I offended you, I'm sorry. OK? There, I
14　　apologized. All right?

15　BILLY: No, it's not all right! If you're going to insult me in
16　　front of the whole team, you ought to apologize to me in
17　　front of the whole team.

18　COACH: Whoa! Stop. Nope. Not going to happen. You're
19　　making way too much out of this.

20　BILLY: Not to me I'm not. (A beat) And just so you know, I
21　　haven't told my parents or the principal or anybody
22　　about what you said, but you don't say something
23　　tomorrow, I'm —

24　COACH: Whoa! Stop! Timeout. Who in the world do you
25　　think you are, kid? I'm the football coach. The *head*

1   football coach! I don't have to apologize to anybody.
2   *Ever.* Not to you, not to your parents, not to anybody. My
3   job is to win football games. And I do whatever I see fit.
4   Understand? Now, I humored you and apologized
5   because you caught me in a good mood. But you're a
6   little grunt freshman, and if you don't like it, you can
7   quit and go do something else. Besides — pfffft — I
8   doubt anybody else remembers what I said, but you.
9   **BILLY:** *(Picking his words carefully)* If you didn't expect them
10   to remember it, then why'd you say it? *(COACH considers*
11   *the determined-looking BILLY for a long moment.)*
12   **COACH:** *(Grunts.)* Obviously ... you've got more *talent* than I
13   thought. Look. Let's do this. *(A beat)* I'll agree to say
14   something at practice tomorrow and you — you agree to
15   forget this people-telling business. OK? *Deal?* *(BILLY*
16   *looks at him for a long moment, then slowly nods his*
17   *agreement and turns and exits. COACH watches him go,*
18   *shakes his head in exasperation, and resumes reading his*
19   *newspaper.)*

Salty

Introduction

Different words often mean different things to different people. That becomes very apparent in this scene as a REPORTER interviews world-famous pirate cook, CHEF Pomperdeux.

1   REPORTER: Chef Pomperdeux, you're noted worldwide for
2   your "salty" language.
3   CHEF: Aye, I am. We pirate chefs tend to be old salty dogs.
4   REPORTER: Well, could you give us an example?
5   CHEF: Sure, when I'm cooking French fries, green beans —
6   *I use salt! Lots of it!* Tomatoes? Salt! Cantaloupe? A
7   favorite — salt! Even me ice cream's got a pinch of the
8   stuff!
9   REPORTER: So, when you refer to being "salty" you're just
10   talking about cooking, right?
11 CHEF: Shiver me timbers, of course I am. What else did you
12   think I was talking about?
13 REPORTER: Well, generally, "salty" language means cussin'
14   and stuff. Dirty words.
15 CHEF: Oh, well ... Sometimes, I do change me language to
16   fit the occasion. For example, if I'm with Brandy, the
17   port wench, I tend to "sugar" me words.
18 REPORTER: Ahhhh ... I see ... to win her heart.
19 CHEF: And if I'm dealing with a fishmonger, I generally
20   "lemon-pepper" my language.
21 REPORTER: All right, that's enough of this idiocy! You're
22   just messin' with me, aren't you, you old "caraway-
23   seed-snorter"?
24 CHEF: Now look here, you little oregano leaf, don't you go
25   using that kind of language with me or I'll give you some

1   **seasoning you'll never forget!** *(They square off with each*
2   *other and get ready for a fight.)*
3   REPORTER: **Well, bring it on, you old cinnamon stick! Just**
4   **wait 'til I rinse your nose out with some Tabasco sauce!**
5   CHEF: **Want to fight dirty, do ya? How about I rub some sea**
6   **salt in your eye?** *(CHEF tosses some sea salt into*
7   *REPORTER's face.)*
8   REPORTER: **Hey, owwww! That's not nice!**
9   CHEF: **Aye, matey. You gotta watch your step if you mix it**
10   **up with us old salty dogs!**

Spontaneous

Introduction
Occasionally, spontaneity does not serve us well as we discover when ROBIN tries to explain to PAT what happened when he finally got to meet the girl of his dreams.

1 ROBIN: Thanks Pat. Thanks for bailing me out of jail, pal. I
2   appreciate it. Sorry.
3 PAT: OK, Robin, let's see if I've got this straight. You went
4   to Neiman Marcus to meet Heidi Crawford? This woman
5   you practically worship, whose pictures hang on every
6   wall in our apartment? *That Heidi Crawford?*
7 ROBIN: *(Small)* Yeah.
8 PAT: And when you got there, you waited in line for *three*
9   *hours?* To meet this woman you adore?
10 ROBIN: *(Smaller)* Uh-huh.
11 PAT: And *then,* when you finally got up to meet her, instead
12   of just shaking her hand, like any civilized person would
13   do, you hauled off and *slugged her in the face?!*
14 ROBIN: *(Lets out a cry of despair.) Ooooh, the travesty of it all!*
15   What have I done? What have I done? I am such a loser!
16 PAT: Dude, your bedroom's a virtual shrine to her! *What*
17   *happened?*
18 ROBIN: I know, I know, I knoooow. *(Sighs, exasperated.)* No,
19   I don't know. It was all just kinda ... spontaneous. I
20   remember standing in line for the longest time and
21   trying to think what I should say to her. I mean, over and
22   over and over, but you know, after a while the thought
23   struck me, "What in the world does a mere mortal like
24   me have to say to this ... this *goddess* of beauty?" I
25   mean, I'm just a dumb schmuck! And then suddenly,

1   there she was, and there I was, and she looked at me,
2   and our eyes met and she was so ... oh, so ... so
3   breathtakingly beautiful, and then she smiled at me and
4   then — then — I don't remember anything after that.
5 PAT: They showed me the videotape at the jail. You're
6   pretty lucky security got you out when they did.
7 ROBIN: I know. I know. *(A beat)* Did I hurt her bad?
8 PAT: Loosened her two front teeth.
9 ROBIN: Ooooh, I am so doomed! Victoria's Secret's gonna
10   hunt me down and kill me! They're going to put me in
11   jail and throw away the key!
12 PAT: Don't feel too bad, dude. Look on the bright side: I bet
13   you made her dentist real happy!

Tricked

Introduction

In this scene, super car salesman ROBIN offers gullible PAT a really hot deal.

1 PAT: You mean, I can have a brand new Audi-T-Forty-Nine
2   for free? You're just going to give it to me? *Brand new?*
3   Not wrecked or nothing? And it's *free?* Nah, there's a
4   catch. What's the catch?
5 ROBIN: No catch. Brand new. Perfect condition. All you
6   have to do is sign this disclaimer, chew up these five
7   little peppers, and the car is yours. *(ROBIN shows PAT a*
8   *little box containing five Red Savina Habanero peppers.)*
9 PAT: Chew them little bitty peppers up, and the car's mine?
10 ROBIN: Yep.
11 PAT: Heck! I'll chew anything for a new car! Where do I sign?
12   This is too easy! What kind of peppers are these? *(ROBIN*
13   *whips out the contract and a pen and PAT signs its.)*
14 ROBIN: Sign right here. They're called Red Savina
15   Habaneros.
16 PAT: Habaneros, huh? Sounds Mexican. OK, hand me one
17   of those bad boys! *(ROBIN holds out the container of*
18   *peppers towards PAT. PAT takes one.)*
19 ROBIN: Here you go. One at time. Whenever you're ready.
20   *(PAT tosses the pepper in his mouth and begins chewing.*
21   *Suddenly, he freezes, he furiously starts spitting and fanning*
22   *his mouth. His eyes tear up and he jumps around in agony.)*
23 PAT: *(Gasping)* Ha — ha — ha — *hot!* I'm on fire! Water,
24   water, water! *(Moaning)* Oh, **Momma!** *(ROBIN hands him*
25   *a glass. PAT gulps it down, but continues in pain.)*

154

1   ROBIN: I hate to tell you this, but water doesn't help. But
2   you can have all you want. You know, according to the
3   Guinness Book of World Records, Habaneros are the
4   second hottest peppers in the world. Whereas your
5   regular run-of-the-mill jalapeno rates about four
6   thousand on the Heat Scale, these little darlings run
7   about five hundred and seventy thousand! *(A beat)* Oh
8   yeah, I forgot. Ready for your *second* one? *(PAT glares at*
9   *ROBIN for a moment in disbelief, moans pathetically, and*
10   *runs Off-Stage. ROBIN watches PAT go, then)* Hmmmm, it
11   looks like he didn't really want the car after all. Oh well.
12   *Who's next?*

Triumphant

Introduction

It's called "leveling the playing field." As this scene begins, JIMMY is having an awful time getting the pesky lid off a jar of pickles. That's when his pal, STUPORMAN, shows up.

1 JIMMY: Man, I wish they didn't put these lids on so tight.

2 STUPORMAN: Here, Jimmy, I'll open it for you.

3 *(STUPORMAN grabs it away from JIMMY and opens it.)*

4 JIMMY: No — wait! Aw, man, I would've had it in a minute.

5 STUPORMAN: Yes, but, unlike you, I can open it — no prob-

6   lem-o!

7 JIMMY: Yeah, thanks, I guess. Say, hey, how come you're

8   hanging around my place so much lately?

9 STUPORMAN: To be quite frank, Jimmy, I had a lot of extra

10   time on my hands. Since I put Flex Fluther away last

11   year, the crime fighting business has gone straight down

12   the tubes. And to top it all off, I think Doris Lane is

13   eyeing that new guy down at the *Weekly Planet*.

14 JIMMY: Gee, that's a bummer.

15 STUPORMAN: Frankly, Jimmy, I've been thinking about

16   dumping this whole Earth business and finding me some

17   new planet to hang around on. I mean, if I'm no use

18   here, what's the point?

19 JIMMY: Gee, Stuporman, that's pretty drastic. Can't you

20   borrow a bad guy from Fatman or Yellow Lantern?

21   They'll share, won't they?

22 STUPORMAN: Nah, they're not working any more than I

23   am. Besides, none of the criminals want to mess with

24   me. They know they can't beat me unless they've got

25   some Kryptonite or something.

1   **JIMMY: Oh, yeah, speaking of Kryptonite, look what I found**
2   **yesterday!** *(JIMMY pulls out a large piece of Kryptonite.)*
3   **STUPORMAN: Ahhhh! Jimmy, get that away from me!**
4   **What are you doing?**
5   **JIMMY: Oh, I just thought it might be interesting to even**
6   **things up a bit, that's all. Here. Let's see you open a jar**
7   ***now!*** *(JIMMY hands STUPORMAN another jar. STUPORMAN*
8   *tries really hard, but he can't get it open. JIMMY takes it away*
9   *from him and opens it himself.)* **Uh-huh, I thought so!**

Uncertainty

Introduction

We all need a hand from time to time as is illustrated in this scene when DR. Jones, an ER doctor, tries to help JEREMY sort through his options during a bad situation.

1 DR: Jeremy, the good news is your mom's going to be OK.
2   We pumped her stomach, gave her some meds. Gave her
3   some charcoal to absorb any drugs we might have
4   missed. Standard procedure. She's going to be OK.
5 JEREMY: No. No, she's not. She hasn't been right since the
6   accident ... not since my dad and sister ... were killed ...
7   she hasn't.
8 DR: Sadly, sometimes after something like that, people
9   can't get past the trauma on their own. They need some
10   help — meds or counseling, or both. *(A beat)* Jeremy,
11   your mom's going to have to go away for a while.
12   Someplace local. And when we get her better, she'll be
13   able to come home, and, hopefully, you guys can go on
14   living your lives. But she's got to do some healing first
15   — inside. *(A beat)* Do you have anybody you can stay
16   with? Any relatives?
17 JEREMY: My grandma, but she's really, really old. Maybe
18   some people at church. I don't know. I don't think I need
19   anybody. I can stay by myself.
20 DR: Now we're not talking a weekend here. We're talking
21   possibly the rest of the school year.
22 JEREMY: I know, I know. Not a problem. I can do it.
23 DR: I'm sure, but legally, I have to call Child Services. What
24   they'll do is come out and check on you, evaluate things,
25   and make sure you're OK. Give you a hand.

1   JEREMY: Whatever. *(A beat)* Do you think Mom's ever going
2   to be OK? Mentally, I mean.
3   DR: I certainly think she can be if she's willing to fight for it
4   and do the work. It may take a while. You never know ...
5   but I do know this: Having a son like you to live for will
6   go a long way towards motivating her to get better.
7   JEREMY: You think?
8   DR: Oh yeah. You don't have any idea just how important
9   you are to her.
10 JEREMY: No, what I don't have is any idea if my momma's
11   ever going to get any better.
12 DR: Yes, she's gonna get better. Let's try not to worry about
13   it. But right now, you look like you could use some
14   supper. Come on. Let's go get you something to eat. My
15   treat.

Witty

Introduction
Oh, the things we do to impress the opposite sex. BO and JO know how.

1 BO: Ha! Ha! Ha!

2 JO: Ha! Ha! Ha! You're so witty.

3 BO: You know it.

4 JO: You're more witty than the kitty from the city.

5 BO: Or a fat cat on the porch mat.

6 JO: The ball in the hall.

7 BO: The stony on the pony.

8 JO: Keep it close to your vest, but you are the best.

9 BO: Not meaning to brag, but in verse I do not lag.

10 JO: Bro, you are so sublime when it comes to rhymes.

11 BO: I only do the best I can, but you know you're the man.

12 JO: But, for all there is to admire, all this is really making
13   me tired.

14 BO: Do say? Give me the re-tread. Tell me about it, Red.

15 JO: I mean always having to say something rhyming is
16   becoming a bore.

17 BO: I'm glad to hear you say that. I was wondering if I was
18   the only ... *one!*

19 JO: You too? Man, what a relief. Now we can just talk
20   normally.

21 BO: But just between the two of us. Nobody else needs to
22   know — especially the girls!

23 JO: Ain't that the truth! To get anywhere with girls you have
24   to be a word wizard.

25 BO: Yeah, they really dig it! Words, words, words.

1   JO: I wonder why?
2   BO: Well, my mom says the way to a man's heart is through
3   his stomach, but my dad says the way to a woman's
4   heart is through her ears.
5   JO: Ain't it the truth, ain't it the truth!

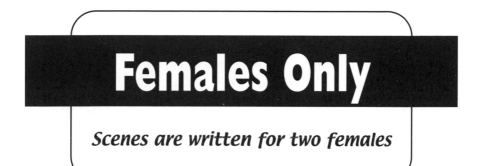

Females Only

Scenes are written for two females

Accidental

Introduction

In this scene, teenager PAT discusses the joys of driving school with her mom, ROBIN.

1 PAT: I love driving! It is so much fun! I clocked in thirty
2   minutes behind the wheel today.
3 ROBIN: I'm glad, dear. And how did Mr. Logan say you did?
4 PAT: Well ... uh ... Mr. Logan didn't say much.
5 ROBIN: Oh, really? Why? He didn't give you any pointers?
6 PAT: No, not really. Mostly, he just held on to the
7   dashboard and mumbled under his breath. Mom, is it
8   natural for your knuckles to turn white when you're
9   squeezing real hard?
10 ROBIN: Uh ... Pat, did something go wrong? What
11   happened?
12 PAT: Well, yes and no. I hit the brakes real quick to avoid
13   hitting a kitty cat as we were going through this
14   intersection —
15 ROBIN: You didn't hit anybody, did you?
16 PAT: No, no, nothing bad like that, Mom.
17 ROBIN: You didn't get rear-ended, did you?
18 PAT: No, but the car behind me did. Luckily, I hit the gas
19   real quick and got out of the way.
20 ROBIN: Oh, dear. Did anybody get hurt?
21 PAT: Not in that car, but I think somebody may have in one
22   of the *other* cars.
23 ROBIN: What *other* cars? How many other cars were
24   involved?
25 PAT: *(Mousey)* Nineteen. Give a car or two.

1   ROBIN: *Nineteen! Patricia!*

2   PAT: It's OK, don't worry, Mom. Really! I didn't get a ticket

3   or anything. I hit the gas and hightailed it out of there. I

4   don't think anybody saw the license plate or anything.

5   ROBIN: Sweetie, they wouldn't have to. "Newton's Drivers

6   Education" is plastered all over the car.

7   PAT: Ooooh, yeah. *(A beat)* Mom, maybe we ought to call a

8   lawyer.

Addiction

Introduction
KISHA has just been caught with her cell phone in class. She scrambles to hide it by sticking it in the back of her pants before her TEACHER can take it.

1 TEACHER: Kisha, give me the cell phone.

2 KISHA: What cell phone? I don't have a cell phone

3 TEACHER: I saw you with the cell phone, please hand it

4   over. You know the school rules.

5 KISHA: But I don't have one.

6 TEACHER: Yes, ma'am, you do. I saw it. Please hand it over.

7   *Now!*

8 KISHA: But I don't have one. Look. *(KISHA holds her hand up*

9   *to show that she doesn't have one.)*

10 TEACHER: Don't do this. Hand it over now or I'm going to

11   have to send you to the office.

12 KISHA: But I don't have one. See! *(KISHA stands up and*

13   *when she does, the cell phone falls out of the back of her*

14   *pants and on to the floor. They both look down at it. KISHA*

15   *scoops it up and holds it tight in her hand.)*

16 TEACHER: See, hand it over.

17 KISHA: No, I can't. I got to have my cell phone. I need my

18   cell phone.

19 TEACHER: Kisha, you know you're not supposed to have it

20   out. Hand it over. I'll give it back at the end of class.

21   *(Hesitantly, KISHA hands over the phone.)*

22 KISHA: You'll give it back? You won't send it to the office?

23 TEACHER: This time. But if you ever refuse to give it to me

24   again or if you lie to me again, it will go to the office.

25 KISHA: But I gotta have my phone. My momma may need

1   to text me. I need my phone. It's my life!
2   TEACHER: No, it's an addiction!
3   KISHA: No, it's my life. I can't live without my life!

Alluring

Introduction
Sometimes you just have to look at the bigger picture —
especially when somebody's trying to grow up.

1 PAT: Jo, those were some pretty interesting vocabulary
2   words you and Julie were working on.
3 JO: Mom! I'm sorry. I didn't know — it was Julie! Not me.
4   Can we just forget it, please? It was nothing. It was just
5   girl talk.
6 PAT: "Sex." "Seduce." "Penis." "Intercourse"!? The way
7   you two were giggling over them, they didn't sound like
8   nothing to me.
9 JO: OK, Mom, you caught us. Guilty as charged! But we
10   weren't really doing anything wrong. They *are* in the
11   dictionary. Besides, I've got to learn this stuff some
12   place.
13 PAT: Yes, but I've always hoped that when you got old
14   enough, you'd come to me for answers. We've always
15   had a good line of communication.
16 JO: Well, you've got to face the facts, Mom. I'm fourteen
17   and I'm growing up. And whether you and Daddy like it
18   or not, there is that *other* side of me!
19 PAT: What other side?
20 JO: You know. My ... earthy side. My sexy side. My alluring
21   side. I do plan for boys to notice me.
22 PAT: Of course you do, but you don't have to accentuate
23   your "earthy side," as you call it, to do that. Boys are
24   going to notice you anyway. You're a pretty girl.
25 JO: Yeah? How?

1   PAT: By simply being yourself. You're sweet and friendly and
2   you've got a good head on your shoulders. Honey, you've
3   got a great personality. And — and you're funny.
4   JO: Yeah, like any of that's ever going to help.
5   PAT: Wait a minute. Something else is going on here. What's
6   really bothering you, sweetie?
7   JO: Well ... there's this new boy at school. Tyler Jones. And
8   I'd like for him to notice me and he won't even look my
9   way. I've tried, but nothing is working.
10 PAT: Aaaah, now I understand.

Believing

Introduction
A crystal ball isn't always necessary to see the future. In this scene, ROBIN helps her blind daughter, PAT, prepare to go to the prom.

1 PAT: How is my dress, Mom? My hair?

2 ROBIN: Perfect, sweetie. You look absolutely beautiful.

3 PAT: Are you sure? I'm so nervous. I can't believe I'm

4   getting to go to the prom.

5 ROBIN: Well, you are and with one of the nicest,

6   handsomest boys in school!

7 PAT: Jimmy is so special.

8 ROBIN: Yes, he is, and he's a very lucky young man 'cause

9   he's getting to go out with my daughter!

10 PAT: On her first date, to the prom!

11 ROBIN: Yes!

12 PAT: And after this, I'm going to graduate and go off to

13   college —

14 ROBIN: And graduate from there and then have a wonderful

15   life!

16 PAT: Do you think so, Momma? There's going to be so many

17   changes.

18 ROBIN: I know so.

19 PAT: So many changes for a blind girl.

20 ROBIN: A lot of changes for any girl. But not any you can't

21   master. Remember, who was it who talked her mother

22   into letting her skydive at twelve and bungee jump at

23   sixteen? That girl can conquer anything else that's

24   waiting for her out there.

25 PAT: Do you truly believe that, Momma? *(The front*

1   *doorbell chimes.)*
2   ROBIN: I do. Hear that? I think somebody's prom date is
3   here. We better get you downstairs.
4   PAT: Thank you, Momma. Thank you for taking care of me
5   my whole life. Thank you for believing in me.
6   ROBIN: Come on. Hurry. We can't keep Jimmy waiting.

Blasé

Introduction

Blasé means to be unconcerned and that pretty much sums up PAT in this scene. Unfortunately, JO doesn't feel that way.

1   JO: You shouldn't have done it.

2   PAT: You really don't seem to have much appreciation for

3   what I've done for you.

4   JO: I *don't!* *(Tearful)* He was my boyfriend.

5   PAT: *Was* is the operative word here. And boyfriends are a

6   dime a dozen for a looker like you. There'll be plenty of

7   others.

8   JO: Maybe so, but this morning, he was the only one I had!

9   PAT: Sweetie, he was no good for you. I did you a favor.

10   JO: Huh? How can you say that? I don't believe you. Pat,

11   you — ran — over — him!

12   PAT: No, Jo, I didn't "run" over him. I didn't run over

13   anybody. Technically, my vehicle veered to the right at a

14   great deal of speed and came in contact with him

15   jogging at a very low rate of speed after which he

16   became airborne for thirty feet and landed on his head.

17   So, actually, I struck him. I didn't run over him.

18   JO: Same difference.

19   PAT: Whatever makes you happy, dear.

20   JO: I hate you. I hate you so much. I hate you more than

21   you could ever know.

22   PAT: Someday, you'll thank me for this.

23   JO: I hope you go to jail. I hope the police come and drag

24   you off and throw you in jail.

25   PAT: Why? It was an accident. All the witnesses said so.

1   Actually, what it was was an "apt opportunity"
2   presenting itself.
3 JO: Don't come home. Don't you ever come home! *(JO exits*
4   *in a huff.)*
5 PAT: She's going to thank me some day. *(A beat)* She will.
6   *(A beat)* I know she will. *(A beat)* Maybe.

Conceited

Introduction
Once again, we learn "pride goes before a fall." In this scene, perfect JO and her world are about to get rocked by imperfect PAT.

1   PAT: Do you like _____? *(Names latest teen heartthrob.)*

2   Oh, I'm sorry, I shouldn't ask. You don't delve into such

3   childish things. You're too mature for that. *(A beat)*

4   What's the nicest gift Gary's ever given you?

5   JO: I don't know. He always has to give me new ones. I'm

6   like a Lamborghini. I must *constantly* be fine-tuned.

7   PAT: Hope Gary's rich. You're pretty high maintenance. See

8   you changed your hair again.

9   JO: Yep. That's right! From brunette to blonde and my eyes

10   are the same way. Today, they're purple. But tomorrow

11   they may be blue or green or violet. It just all depends

12   on my mood. And why not? Not everybody wants to be

13   as simple as you are Pat.

14 PAT: Yeah, that's me. "Simple" Pat, and you're

15   "Kaleidoscope" Jo, 'cause nobody knows how you're

16   going to look the next time they see you.

17 JO: Darn right about that. I like to mess with people's

18   minds that way. *(PAT's phone rings. She pulls it out.)*

19 PAT: Hello? *(Listens.)* Oh, hi. *(Listens.)* Casting Crowns?

20   Really? Oh, I'd love to. Thanks. *(PAT hangs up her phone*

21   *and gathers up her purse and jacket and heads for the door.)*

22   Sorry, Jo, I gotta run. I just got asked to go to the

23   Casting Crowns concert tonight! I gotta go get ready!

24   Bye!

25 JO: OK. Bye! *(In a subdued voice)* Have a good time. *(JO*

1   *pulls out her phone and dials.)* **I wonder why Gary isn't**
2   **taking me to the concert?** *(After someone picks up the*
3   *other line)* **Gary? Gary! I was just talking to Pat and she's**
4   **going to the Casting Crowns concert. How come we're**
5   **not going to the Casting Crowns concert?** *(She listens*
6   *some more.)* **What! What do you mean 'cause you're going**
7   **with Pat?! What —** *(Listens again.)* **What do you mean I**
8   **probably wouldn't like it? It doesn't matter if I wouldn't**
9   **like it or not. The point is to be seen there by all the right**
10   **people.** *(Click! Gary hangs up on her.)* **Gary? Gary? Gary!**
11   *(She flips her phone shut, lets out a huff, and stomps out of*
12   *the room. Calling off)* **Mom!**

Curious

Introduction

If curiosity didn't kill the cat, it at least ruined her day! In this scene, sisters JO and PAT are snooping around in the garage where JO thinks their dad has something to hide.

1 PAT: We shouldn't be doing this! If Daddy finds out we're
2   out here snooping in his stuff, he'll ground us forever.
3 JO: Relax! Him and Mom are gone to the mall. OK? We're
4   just going to look. We're not going to take anything.
5 PAT: So, what happened again?
6 JO: I walked out here while he was looking at something in
7   this box and when I said, "Whatchaya doin'?" he just
8   about jumped out of his skin and slammed this lid really
9   fast.
10 PAT: You startled him. Look, the lid's not even locked. Can't
11   be anything in there too bad.
12 JO: Well, we're fixing to find out. *(JO starts to open the box.*
13   *PAT puts her hand on top of the box.)*
14 PAT: Jo, don't! This is wrong. We shouldn't do this! Listen,
15   hear me out: I'm sure there's not any great bad, dark
16   secret in this box, but just on the outside chance, *what*
17   *if there is?* I mean, do we really want to know that about
18   our dad? There's some things I'd just as soon not know
19   about.
20 JO: Like what? You mean, you're afraid dear old pop may be
21   a closet alcoholic, or a drug addict, or maybe — maybe
22   — he's having an affair on the side and he's hiding his
23   girlfriend's phone number out here in this box? Or — or
24   — or worst yet, maybe *this* is where he hides his stash
25   of — dirty magazines!

1   PAT: Joanne Dannon Lewis, you are wicked! Have you ever
2   seen anything — *anything* — that would make you think
3   our daddy is into anything like that? Have you? *Have*
4   *you?*
5   JO: *(Gleefully)* **Nope! But we're fixing to find out!** *(JO throws*
6   *open the box lid and both GIRLS stare down the box for a*
7   *moment. Then, JO reaches down and brings out a small*
8   *jewelry case. They exchange looks. She then opens it up and*
9   *lifts out a necklace. PAT takes hold of the pendant dangling*
10   *at the end of the chain and examines it.)*
11 PAT: **Hmmmm? I wonder whose name around here starts**
12   **with the letter ... J?** *(JO abruptly pulls the pendant away*
13   *from her and quickly repacks everything back into the box.*
14   *PAT grins at her sheepishly. Perky)* **Well, I guess we know**
15   **what** *you're* **getting on your birthday!**

Energetic

Introduction
"Pudgy" is in the eyes of the beholder, right? In this scene, PAT watches JO as she goes through a series of rigorous exercises. JO never stops working out as they talk.

1 PAT: Whoa, Jo. I've never seen you so energized.
2 JO: Yep. You lose one hundred and thirty pounds and you'd
3   be energized, too.
4 PAT: Well, I've never needed to lose that much weight, but
5   I've still never had as much energy as you've got right
6   now.
7 JO: Maybe it's because you've never really appreciated what
8   you had. I mean, I've never been able to move this easy
9   or run this easy before in my life.
10 PAT: Yep, you've come a long way. You look good. Act like
11   you feel good.
12 JO: I do feel good and I do have more energy. Come on, jog
13   with me.
14 PAT: Nah. I think I'll pass.
15 JO: It'll tone your muscles up. Expand your lungs. Give *you*
16   more energy!
17 PAT: No, I'm happy where I am.
18 JO: You don't want to improve?
19 PAT: It's not that I don't want to improve, it's just that I
20   don't *need* to improve.
21 JO: What do you mean? We all need to improve. Are you
22   saying only fat people need to improve?
23 PAT: No. Not exactly. I'm just saying that some of us are
24   OK just the way we are.
25 JO: In other words, if you've never been fat, you're

1   automatically OK?

2   PAT: No, I'm just comfortable with myself. Who I am now.

3   Where I am. I don't need to do what you're doing.

4   JO: Well, I like where I am right now and I'm going to stay

5   this way! See you later, pudgy! *(JO turns away and jogs*

6   *Off-Stage.)*

7   PAT: Pudgy? Who are you calling pudgy? Hey, wait up! Bet

8   I can beat you around the block!

Enthusiastic

Introduction
Enthusiasm is good, but let's be reasonable, OK? In this scene, a teacher-sponsor interviews a slightly wired prospective cheerleader.

1 **PAT: Jo! Jo, come over here and have a seat. You did great!**
2 **JO: Thanks, Mrs. May.** *(JO immediately strikes a pose and*
3 *then continues doing cheers. Cheerleader loud)* **Push 'em**
4 **back! Push 'em back! Waaaay back!**
5 **PAT: My, Jo, I must say, that was the most enthusiastic**
6 **tryout I think we've ever had.**
7 **JO: Really? Great.** *(Another yell)* **Goooo, Cadets!**
8 **PAT: Ah, yes. Well, now, there's something we need to run**
9 **over before —**
10 **JO:** *(Another yell)* **Rrrrun-run-run it in!** *(Normal voice)* **Sorry.**
11 **I'm a little worked up.**
12 **PAT: Yes ... as I was saying, we need to run over some**
13 **things before you can become a cheerleader.**
14 **JO:** *(Another yell)* **Through the air, on the ground, goooo**
15 **team!**
16 **PAT: OK, Jo. You can stop now. Thanks. The auditions are**
17 **over.**
18 **JO: I know, but,** *(In cheer voice)* **our team has got to go-go-**
19 **go!**
20 **PAT: Jo, are you OK?**
21 **JO:** *(In cheer voice)* **Whatdya think? Whatdya think? Put 'em**
22 **in the kitchen sink!**
23 **PAT:** *(In a worried voice)* **Joooo?**
24 **JO:** *(In cheer voice)* **We're OK, we're OK! Take that ball the**
25 **other way!**

1   **PAT: Let me guess, you hyped up on Red Bull before you**
2   **tried out, right? How many cans?**
3   **JO:** *(A little cry)* **Yes!** *(Then, in cheer voice)* **Five, five, alive! We**
4   **don't take no stinkin' jive!**
5   **PAT: Five cans, huh? Whoa.** *(Gets out cell phone and dials.)*
6   **I'm calling your parents.**
7   **JO:** *(In cheer voice)* **Don't wanna lose, don't wanna flop, call**
8   **me some help, 'cause I can't stop!**

Fired

Introduction
Think your day's been bad? Wait until you hear about PAT's!

1   PAT: *Aaaagh!* Mom, this is the worst day of my life! I've
2   dreamed of being a Disney mermaid all my life, and
3   when I finally get to be one, I get fired!
4   ROBIN: Fired? You got fired? Honey, what happened?
5   PAT: It was my costume. Maybe I got the wrong suit — I
6   don't know. It just came apart!
7   ROBIN: Came apart? You mean your mermaid outfit?
8   PAT: Yeah. Right in the middle of the Swoop Maneuver!
9   ROBIN: The Swoop Maneuver?
10 PAT: You know. That part where we have to do that quick
11   deep-divey move thing, and then that little twisty move,
12   and then we all shoot back up to the top? Well, when I
13   did it, the whole outfit just peeled off of me like I was a
14   banana!
15 ROBIN: How awful!
16 PAT: And that's not even the worst of it! We were doing a
17   special performance for the Vienna Boy's Choir! So there
18   I was, shooting straight up for the top when I suddenly
19   felt wetter than usual and I looked down and my — my
20   — my tail was gone!
21 ROBIN: Oh, dear! What did you do then?
22 PAT: I screamed! Except you can't scream under water so I
23   inhaled about a gallon of water, and I thought I was
24   going to drown, but it was too late!
25 ROBIN: Too late?

1 PAT: *(Defeated)* Yeah. Mother, do you know what happens
2   when three hundred fat little Venetians all scream high C
3   at the same time? They shatter glass.
4 ROBIN: You don't mean — !?
5 PAT: Yep, the whole front panel of the aquarium shook,
6   cracked, and collapsed! And fifteen mermaids and fifty
7   thousand gallons of water gushed into the auditorium!
8   And me? I ended up lying naked across the laps of a half
9   dozen sex-crazed pubescent Austrians! Oh, Momma it
10   was so embarrassing!
11 ROBIN: Now, now, come here and let Momma hold you. It'll
12   be OK. *(A beat)* Of course, you know that, actually, they
13   were Viennese, not Venetians. Venetians are window
14   shades.

Frustration

Introduction
It's springtime and prom dresses are busting out all over — just ask BETTY and VERONICA!

1 BETTY: Here. This is it. This is the one!

2 VERONICA: Oh, yeah, Betty. That's it. That looks great. It's

3   so hot.

4 BETTY: Will you help me zip it up in the back?

5 VERONICA: Sure thing. *(VERONICA attempts to zip it up some*

6   *more, but it won't go up.)* Uh ... I ... man, Betty, it won't

7   go.

8 BETTY: No! It has to go. Try harder.

9 VERONICA: I am trying harder. It won't budge.

10 BETTY: Shoot! I knew something like this would happen!

11 VERONICA: Have you put on a little weight?

12 BETTY: *(Nattily)* No! I haven't put on any weight and I resent

13   the implication.

14 VERONICA: Sorry. Sorry. Maybe they've got it in a bigger

15   size.

16 BETTY: No. She said this is the only one they've got.

17 VERONICA: Bummer.

18 BETTY: Great! Find the one dress I like and it doesn't fit. I

19   can't believe this. *(BETTY reaches back and tries to zip up*

20   *the dress herself. She grunts as she tries.)*

21 VERONICA: I don't think it's going to work.

22 BETTY: Shut up, Veronica! You're not helping.

23 VERONICA: Sorry. Sorry. Don't blame me. I'm not the one

24   who's gotten bigger.

25 BETTY: The only place I've gotten bigger is here. *(BETTY*

1   *motions to her bust line.)*
2   **VERONICA: Well, the boys'll like that.**
3   **BETTY: Ooooh, I can't believe you!** *You* **are absolutely no**
4   **help!**

Guarantees

Introduction
Sometimes it's the simplest things that make life bearable. In this scene, a mother and a daughter deal with the daunting prospect of facing brain surgery.

1 ALEEAH: Mom! I don't want them shaving my head!
2   Couldn't they just shave a spot? Just where they're — ?
3 MOM: No, Aleeah. They have to shave it all. *(A long silence.)*
4 ALEEAH: But I can get a wig, right?
5 MOM: Sure. Any color you want.
6 ALEEAH: Purple?
7 MOM: Purple? *That* I don't know. *(They laugh together. Then*
8   *there is another long silence.)*
9 ALEEAH: They're going to get all of it, aren't they? The
10   tumor?
11 MOM: Oh, sure. Between the surgery and radiation, it's all
12   going away.
13 ALEEAH: You think we'll get all of this done in time for me
14   to go to prom, Mom?
15 MOM: Aleeah, honey, I don't know. We're just going to have
16   to wait and see.
17 ALEEAH: Is there going to be a scar? Am I going to end up
18   looking weird or something?
19 MOM: No, silly. Once your hair grows back, nobody'll ever
20   know. Unless you show them.
21 ALEEAH: *(After a beat)* This is going to stop the seizures,
22   right?
23 MOM: The doctors think so. We wouldn't let them do this if
24   we didn't think so.
25 ALEEAH: But there's no guarantee?

1   MOM: Sweetie, we both know there's no guarantees in life.
2   ALEEAH: *(ALEEAH nods her understanding and then stares at*
3   *the floor, thinking. Finally)* **Then I can get the purple one,**
4   **right?**
5   MOM: A purple one? Are you sure? Oh, all right. If we can
6   get that past your daddy!

Happiness

Introduction
In this scene, JO helps PAT gain a new perspective on what true happiness really is.

1 PAT: *(Excited)* Jo! Jo, guess what? I am so happy. I just got
2   ... a brand new car! My daddy bought me a new _____
3   *(Fill in with the latest hot car).*
4 JO: Wow, that's great.
5 PAT: And to top it all off: Tonight, I'm going to the
6   _____ *(Fill in with the latest hot band)* concert and
7   I've got backstage passes so I get to hang out with the
8   band after the concert!
9 JO: That's terrific!
10 PAT: And this morning, I got my acceptance letter from
11   Harvard — my first school of choice.
12 JO: Fantastic!
13 PAT: And my prom dress? I got it yesterday. Oh. My. Gosh.
14   It's soooo beautiful. I look at it and almost cry. I am
15   soooo, soooo happy.
16 JO: That's great. What color is it?
17 PAT: Oh, it's pink with a chiffon trim and — oh, wait, just
18   listen to me? I'm such a blabbermouth. I haven't even
19   asked you about your day. How has your day been?
20 JO: Well ... I went to St. Jude's this morning to see my
21   cancer doctor and found out that I've probably got a year
22   to live instead of the six months they gave me the last
23   time I was there. I'm pretty stoked about that.
24 PAT: *(Completely stunned)* Oh my gosh, oh my gosh! Jo! Jo,
25   I — I am so sorry. I didn't know. What have you got?

189

1   Does it hurt?

2   JO: Nah. It's OK. Nobody knows. It's a brain tumor. Pretty

3   deep. They can't really do anything for it. You're the first

4   person I've told. I haven't wanted to be everybody's

5   object to pity my senior year. My eyesight got screwy.

6   That's how they found it. At some point, I may start

7   having seizures so if you see me flopping around on the

8   floor, you'll know what's happening. But it's not growing

9   as fast as they thought it would so that's pretty good.

10 PAT: A year? Wow. *(A beat)* Oh my gosh, oh my gosh, then

11   we really *do* have something to be happy about, don't

12   we? Yeah ... That's something ... I mean ... Hey! Have

13   you got your prom dress yet? Because if you haven't, I'd

14   consider it a real honor if you'd let me help you pick one

15   out, and then — then I'd like to pay for it! And *that's*

16   what would really make me happy!

Maturity

Introduction
Part of being mature is knowing better than to play with fire. This scene begins with new teenage mom, PAT, and her own mother standing over the baby bed of their child and grandchild.

1 PAT: Mom, I can't do this. I can't take care of him.

2 MOM: Yes, you can. You have to. You've always been crazy
3   about the idea of having a baby and now you've got one.

4 PAT: But I don't know what to do and he cries all the time.

5 MOM: Honey, part of being an adult is putting up with the
6   hard times and doing what's best for the ones depending
7   on you even when you're hurting. That's called maturity.

8 PAT: Then I'm not mature, OK? I can't do this.

9 MOM: I wish you'd thought of that before you decided to
10   have this baby.

11 PAT: I didn't decide to have this baby!

12 MOM: You decided to have sex!

13 PAT: *That's not the same!* OK, I get it. OK? I goofed. I
14   messed up. How long do I have to carry this cross?

15 MOM: I don't know. For the next eighteen years, I guess.

16 PAT: OK, Mom, I get it. I screwed up. Alright? But right now
17   I need some help with this baby.

18 MOM: What do you expect me to do?

19 PAT: Help me! I don't know what to do. Please, Momma!

20 MOM: No. I'm not going to help you! I didn't sign up for this.
21   I've raised my kids. I'm not going to raise my grandkids
22   because of your irresponsibility. You got yourself in this
23   mess, you can get yourself out.

24 PAT: Mother! Didn't you just say maturity was doing what's
25   best for the ones you love even when you're hurting?

1 **Little Charlie is hurting, Mom! Help him! I don't know**
2 **how to help him! Don't let him hurt because of my**
3 **mistake. I goofed, he didn't.** *(Crying)* **Please, Momma.**
4 **Help us. Please.**
5 **MOM:** *(Sighs.)* **OK. Let's see what he needs.** *(MOM reaches*
6 *down into the crib.)*

Organized

Introduction
In this scene, SUZY, a soon-to-be bride, gives her friend JILL a tour of her very organized newlywed apartment. JILL has just opened a pantry door to look at the canned goods.

1 SUZY: I came over every day this last week and worked on
2   organizing everything. The kitchen. The closets. The
3   bathroom. That way, when we get back from Honolulu,
4   the apartment will be all ready for us.
5 JILL: Did you do this? *(JILL holds out a tin can with no label*
6   *on it.)* Take all the labels off the canned goods?
7 SUZY: What? Let me see. Oh, my gosh. They've taken all
8   the labels off! I can't believe — *who did this?* Now, how
9   — how am I going to know what I'm opening?
10 JILL: I guess you won't. It'll be "cook's surprise"!
11 SUZY: No! No! I can't deal with this. This is too much.
12 JILL: Oh, Suzy, it's just a joke. Lighten up. This gets done
13   to lots of newlyweds.
14 SUZY: But not to me. I had everything in place. I had it
15   organized. I had it *all* organized!
16 JILL: Oh, loosen up, Miss Suzy Homemaker. We've got a
17   wedding tomorrow night!
18 SUZY: But — who — who could have done this? Oh, no! You
19   don't think they messed with the rest of the apartment,
20   do you? *(SUZY rushes off. A moment later, she screams. A*
21   *beat later, she stumbles back in, dazed.)* Oh, no! It's ruined!
22   The whole place! The closet. The bathroom. They look
23   like a tornado's hit!
24 JILL: Come on, Suzy, I'm sure it'll be OK.
25 SUZY: I'm a failure. How's Todd gonna love a wife who can't

1   even organize their own home?
2   JILL: Oh, stop! You're overthinking this thing, Suzy, Todd's
3   a guy. I'm sure your organizational skills are not at the
4   top of his list of reasons for loving you. Do you think?
5   SUZY: You mean, if I keep him ... *distracted,* he won't notice
6   the mess until I can get it cleaned up?
7   JILL: You keep him "distracted" and he'll think he's still in
8   Hawaii!

Patience

Introduction

Patience is a virtue. But maybe not always? In this scene, we find the Jones family having a picnic near the rim of the Grand Canyon until —

1 PAT: Mommy! Mommy!

2 ROBIN: What is it, honey? What's happened?

3 PAT: It's Tommy, Momma! He fell!

4 ROBIN: Fell? Where?

5 PAT: Over the edge!

6 ROBIN: Over the edge? You mean he's fallen into the

7   canyon? Oh, no! Where?

8 PAT: Here! *(They both rush to the edge of the canyon and peer*

9   *down over the rim.)* **He's still falling, Momma. He hasn't**

10   **hit the side or anything.** *(Amazed)* **Look, Momma, he's**

11   **waving at us.** *(They both wave down to him.)*

12 ROBIN: Oh, my goodness! Sure is a long way down there. I

13   never realized it was so deep.

14 PAT: The brochure said seven hundred feet! *(ROBIN turns*

15   *away and calls off for help.)*

16 ROBIN: Help! Help! Somebody help us! *(A beat)* Nobody

17   seems to be around. No park rangers. Nobody.

18 PAT: Look, Momma! He's pulled his homework out of his

19   backpack and started working on it.

20 ROBIN: Ooooh, that boy! Just like your brother to pull a

21   stupid stunt like this and try to ruin our picnic, but I'll

22   tell you what. *(ROBIN returns to the picnic spread and starts*

23   *preparing food. PAT comes over and joins her.)* **While we're**

24   **waiting, why don't we break out this picnic basket, what**

25   **do you say? I'm famished! I reckon we'll hear a thud or**

1   something when he hits bottom.

2   PAT: I bet ya a dollar it's more of a *splat!*

3   ROBIN: Maybe so, maybe so. Care for a chicken leg?

Plain

Introduction

This scene is done with apologies to Plain, Wisconsin. We enter this scene with JO helping PAT get ready for her first beauty pageant.

1 PAT: You think I can win? I've never been in a pageant
2   before.
3 JO: Absolutely. I've been in tons. It's a piece of cake. Walk.
4   Smile. Wave. Don't fall down.
5 PAT: These earrings?
6 JO: No, too fancy. Try these. *(JO hands her another pair. PAT*
7   *puts them on. JO continues to hand her different items.)*
8 PAT: This necklace?
9 JO: A bit much. Use this one.
10 PAT: This eye shadow? Does it go with this lipstick?
11 JO: Too much. Let's take a tissue to those. Tone it down a
12   little.
13 PAT: There. How's that?
14 JO: Better.
15 PAT: Look at me. Do you think I really have a chance?
16 JO: With this a-line dress you sewed yourself? You're a
17   shoo-in!
18 PAT: Oh, no, my shoes! I almost forgot. The Pradas or the
19   Reeboks?
20 JO: Definitely the Reeboks. Oh, yeah. The high-tops! Nice
21   touch. Extra points there.
22 PAT: This bow?
23 JO: Oh, yeah. The bigger the better. *(PAT finishes dressing*
24   *and moves out to the middle of the floor.)*
25 PAT: OK. How do I look?

1   JO: You — look — uh — uh — plain.
2   PAT: *(Excited)* Oh, do I?
3   JO: Yep. I think you've got the Miss Plain Pageant in the
4   bag!

Remorseful

Introduction

What do you do when it all *really does* go wrong? Sadly, in this scene, SHIRLEY gets to find out.

1 WANDA: You're disgusting!

2 SHIRLEY: Wanda, I'm sorry. It was an accident.

3 WANDA: No-no-no-no! Don't even start that! There's no way

4   in the world you take my dress without asking, wear it

5   to a party, and then "accidently" hook up with my

6   boyfriend! Uh-uh, nothin' accidental about that.

7 SHIRLEY: But it was. I mean, hooking up with Nick. I never

8   intended that to happen.

9 WANDA: Keep talkin'. You ain't digging your way out of this

10   hole, girlfriend. You stole my dress!

11 SHIRLEY: No! No. I just borrowed it.

12 WANDA: What you did was you snuck into my closet when

13   I was gone, took my dress, wore it to a party, and then

14   had the gall to bring it back and hang it in my closet as

15   if nothin' had even happened! Did you think he wouldn't

16   tell me?

17 SHIRLEY: No.

18 WANDA: Or that nobody at school would tell me, either? Are

19   you that stupid?

20 SHIRLEY: I guess so. It's just that ... I mean ... I didn't ...

21   I ... just ... didn't ...

22 WANDA: *Think?* You're sure right about that and you got

23   caught and now you're sorry!

24 SHIRLEY: But I *am* sorry. And not just because I got

25   caught. It was all so wrong. I guess ... I guess I was

1   jealous. You're so pretty. You've always had a boyfriend.
2   I've never had anybody. And I thought ... I didn't think
3   anything would happen. Never in a million years.
4   WANDA: Well, it did! And in my dress! And with my
5   boyfriend! And now it's over between him and me! And
6   it's all because of you!
7   SHIRLEY: Oh, Wanda, please! Forgive me!
8   WANDA: Nah-uh! You stay away from me, girl. You're bad
9   news. That's what you are. Just stay away from me and
10   don't ever talk to me again! *(WANDA walks away.)*
11 SHIRLEY: Oh, Wanda, please!

Scary

Introduction

In this scene, LISA and TRISA discover that some real things are scarier than the monsters in the movies.

1   LISA: *(A loud whisper)* He's in there! *I know it!* I know I've
2   got to go in there, but will you go with me? I'm terrified.
3   TRISA: Of course I will, silly. But you have to go first.
4   LISA: Why?
5   TRISA: Because you're the one getting paid for this,
6   remember? I'm not.
7   LISA: Oh, yeah. I forgot. Babysitting — yuck! I hate it. *(A*
8   *beat)* Listen. It's in there waiting. Gurgling. Waiting.
9   Drooling.
10 TRISA: Stop it! You're scaring me now.
11 LISA: Am I? Good. *(A beat)* There. I think I heard it again.
12   Did you hear it?
13 TRISA: Nah. What did ya hear?
14 LISA: You know. That sound it makes when it's — it's —
15 TRISA: Making more?
16 LISA: Yeah. That's it: *(Ominously) making more!*
17 TRISA: Gosh! You've got to do something. It's time you
18   dealt with this once and for all.
19 LISA: I can't! I can't! Please. Please, don't make me!
20 TRISA: Lisa! Look at me. Look at me. You've put this off
21   long enough. Go in there and face it now or lose every
22   shred of self-respect you've ever had!
23 LISA: You're right. I've got to do this. OK. Wish me luck.
24   Here I go. *(LISA opens the door and rushes in. TRISA stands*
25   *waiting at the door. Suddenly, we hear LISA scream and in*

1   *a moment she comes running back out. She holds her hands*
2   *away from her body as if they have been contaminated.*
3   *Wailing)* **Oh, my gosh,** *it's — so — so —* **bad!** **It's**
4   **everywhere!** *Everywhere!* **What am I going to do?** *Poop!*
5   *Poop!* **Ohhhh, yuck! I've got baby poop on my hands!** *(In*
6   *a demented voice)* **You and your big ideas! Come here.** *Let*
7   *— me — share! (LISA tries to wipe her hands on TRISA.*
8   *TRISA screams and exits Off-Stage. LISA follows her.)*

Searching

Introduction
Here's a new twist on the old saying, "Seeing eye to eye." JO is having serious issues prior to her prom date's arrival.

1 JO: Mom! Bobby's going to be here any minute and I can't
2   find it!
3 MOM: Relax honey, we'll find it.
4 JO: But what if we don't? I can't go to the prom like this.
5   I'll be the only one there with an eye patch!
6 MOM: Jo, relax, we'll find your glass eye.
7 JO: The blue one. I don't want to be the only one there with
8   one blue eyeball and one green one!
9 MOM: OK! Did you check the bathroom? Where's the last
10   place you had it?
11 JO: If I could remember that, Mom, I'd know where it was.
12 MOM: I was just asking. I'll look in Timmy's room. *(MOM*
13   *exits. There is the sound of a car horn honking outside.)*
14 JO: Oh, no! Mom! He's here! *(Calling downstairs)* **Dad! Stall**
15   **him at the door!** *(To herself)* **Oh, great! The biggest night**
16   **of my life and I'm going to be either Cindy Cyclops or**
17   **Little Mismatched Eye Girl!** *(MOM reenters.)*
18 MOM: All right, I found it. You can calm down.
19 JO: Where was it?
20 MOM: In the middle of some clay man Timmy was making.
21 JO: *(Calling off)* **I hate you, Timmy!**
22 MOM: Stop. Leave your little brother alone. If you hadn't left
23   it lying around, he wouldn't have picked it up. Here. I
24   **washed it off.** *(JO takes the eye and pops it back into her*
25   *eye socket.)*

1   JO: There. How do I look?

2   MOM: Beautiful. Just beautiful!

Sensible

Introduction
Just how "sensible" should a girl be when she's out shopping for clothes?

1   *(The scene begins with PAT holding out two pairs of shoes for*
2   *ROBIN to look at.)*
3   PAT: I shouldn't get these shoes even though they'll go with
4   my outfit better? *(Referring to the other pair)* **These are the**
5   **more sensible ones to get because they're cheaper? Is**
6   **that what you're saying?**
7   ROBIN: Yeah, that's what I think. Those are nice, but
8   they're way overpriced. Got to keep within your budget,
9   remember?
10 PAT: Yes, I know. But Robin, everything I've picked out so
11   far ... the purse I liked was too big, the dress was "too
12   young looking." Isn't that what you said? Everything I've
13   picked out so far, you haven't liked. None of it has been
14   "sensible" to you.
15 ROBIN: I'm only trying to help. If you didn't want my
16   opinion, why'd you ask me to come along?
17 PAT: I didn't! You invited yourself when I told you I was
18   going shopping.
19 ROBIN: Look, I've just been trying to help you make some
20   sensible choices that will look good on you. It's not my
21   fault that your fashion sense is zilch.
22 PAT: And yours is one hundred and eight, right?
23 ROBIN: I know, I'm gifted. Sometimes it's a burden, but I
24   do try to help the less gifted. *(PAT looks at ROBIN for a*
25   *long moment. She then puts down the pair of shoes she was*

1   *holding and picks up the pair she had originally wanted.)*
2   PAT: Well, that's very "sensible" of you, Robin. I do like to
3   be "sensible," too. In fact, I like to do sensible things
4   that are going to help save the planet and, you know, I
5   think the sensible thing for me to do today is to just let
6   you ride the city bus home. It stops only two blocks from
7   your house. Makes more sense than me wasting my
8   expensive gas to take you there.
9   ROBIN: Now wait a minute! Let's not go overboard on this
10   "being sensible" stuff. We've got to use a little common
11   sense here!
12   PAT: Common sense? What's that? Hmmmm?! My common
13   sense tells me I *do* want that dress, even though it's
14   "too young" for me, and ditto on that designer purse
15   even though it is "too big." And the shoes? *My*
16   sensibilities tell me that I deserve them for having *put up*
17   *with you* on this shopping trip! What does your common
18   sense say?
19   ROBIN: It says, "OK, OK," just as long as you don't make
20   me ride the bus home.

Sentimental

Introduction

Some parents seem to dote on their children, so when they leave home to go to college it is hard — on both the kids and the parents, or so it seems.

1 DOT: Mom! No! Not again.

2 MOM: What? I can't look at your baby pictures?

3 DOT: Sure you can. Just don't do it now. Mom!

4   Graduation's tonight. Monday, I'm leaving for college.

5   Couldn't you just put this off a day or two until I'm

6   gone? Please?

7 MOM: Why?

8 DOT: 'Cause you always get so mushy about them, so

9   sentimental! You start sighing, then it's *(Mimicking her)*

10   "Oh, how sweet" and "My little-babey-wabey," and then

11   you start crying.

12 MOM: Oh, stop it. I do not. You're exaggerating. Besides,

13   look at these! *(MOM starts thumbing through a photo*

14   *album. She points out different pictures.)* **Here you are in my**

15   **daddy's arms. Three months old.** *(Sighs.)* **He loved you**

16   **so much. And look at this one — your first tooth. And**

17   **here's your fourth birthday party. Oh, how sweet.**

18 DOT: Mom. You're starting! Don't do it!

19 MOM: And here — here you are in your little white Easter

20   outfit. And this one — *(Choking up)* Ohhhh, my little-

21   baby-wabey. You've grown up so fast and *(Wailing)* now

22   you're leaving home!

23 DOT: Forty miles, Mom. *Forty miles!* I'll be back every other

24   weekend to do laundry. Look, Mom, Tommy's out in the

25   car. I gotta go up to the school. Are you going to be OK?

1   MOM: *(Drying up her tears)* **Yes, yes. Go on. Go on. I'll be OK.**
2   **Fine.**
3   DOT: **You sure? Now, I've got my cell phone so if you need**
4   **me you call me OK? Bye, Mom.** *(DOT exits. MOM waves*
5   *good-bye, watches her go, then wipes her tears as she grabs*
6   *her cell phone and flips it open. She dials and listens for an*
7   *answer on the other end.)*
8   MOM: *(Into the phone)* **Dorothy? Jane. Yeah, she's gone.**
9   **Yours?** *(Listening)* **Good. Right. Right. Oh, brother! The**
10   **things we do for our kids. So, now, tell me about this**
11   **cruise we're going on next month?**

Soaked

Introduction
Ah, falling in love, ain't it wet ... er ... we mean grand!

1   *(ROBIN, covered in some gooey liquid, enters PAT's kitchen.)*

2   PAT: Robin! Come in, come in. Ah, man, look at you. You're

3   covered!

4   ROBIN: I know. I'm sorry. Ooooh, it's just dripping off of

5   me.

6   PAT: You really fell into it, didn't you? Here, stand on this

7   towel so you don't drip all over the floor.

8   ROBIN: Yuck! My mom is going to kill me.

9   PAT: Relax. Don't be so hard on yourself. You know, you're

10   not the first person in the world to "fall" into love. It's

11   quite the goo. And don't forget, your mom must have

12   fallen into it herself sometime or other or you wouldn't

13   be here.

14   ROBIN: Maybe so, but I bet I'm the first one to almost

15   drown in it.

16   PAT: No, no, no. Not quite.

17   ROBIN: Who would have imagined it? Me — falling in love. I

18   wonder if Tide will take this out. Maybe bleach. Here,

19   help me out of this.

20   PAT: Nope, no can do. You gotta do that yourself. Nobody

21   can help you, but you. That's what happens when you

22   fall into love.

23   ROBIN: But, it's soooo sticky. *(Sniffs.)* Smells sweet,

24   though.

25   PAT: Sweetest thing in the world! And often it stays that

1   way, but not always. Sometimes it goes sour on you.
2   Sometimes even acidic. Can eat a hole in your heart.
3   See. Here's my scar. *(PAT pulls down the front of her shirt*
4   *a little to expose a scar on her chest.)*
5 ROBIN: Oh, Pat, you fell in love once, too? I didn't know
6   that.
7 PAT: A couple of years ago. I don't like to talk about it.
8 ROBIN: Oh, girl, I am sorry.
9 PAT: Not to worry. I'm over it. But falling in love doesn't
10   always do that to you. Sometimes, you get soaked in it
11   and it's just like bathing in happiness!
12 ROBIN: That's what I'm hoping for.
13 PAT: Yeah, me too.

Teasing

Introduction
You go to college to get an education. In this scene, PAT is enrolled in College 101: Read the Label before Consuming!

1 PAT: It's. Not. Funny. *(She pukes into the commode.)*
2 ROBIN: Oh, don't worry. I'm not laughing at you. I'm
3   laughing at what you did.
4 PAT: You know *a friend* would have told me that I was eating
5   dog food instead of chili!
6 ROBIN: I know. Sorry. I was just curious to see how far
7   you'd go before you realized your mistake.
8 PAT: I hate him. I hate that *dog*. *(She pukes some more.)*
9 ROBIN: Now, now, don't blame the dog.
10 PAT: But I do! The little beast got in the cabinet and
11   switched all the cans around!
12 ROBIN: Nemo is pretty smart. But I don't know if he's *that*
13   smart.
14 PAT: He's not smart: he's *evil!*
15 ROBIN: Oh, now, just because you don't love Alpo doesn't
16   mean the dog is out to get you.
17 PAT: You don't know do you? You have no idea? What he
18   does when we're not here?
19 ROBIN: What are you — ? He runs around, chases his tail,
20   and barks out the window.
21 PAT: No! He does other does things. Evil things! The roast
22   that disappeared last week? He ate it and stuffed the
23   plastic wrap between my sheets! And our clothes? You
24   know how they've been looking so ratty? It's 'cause he's
25   been chewing on them while we're gone. And not only

211

1   that, when I came home early last week, guess what I
2   caught him doing? Wearing *your* clothes! He had on your
3   pink blouse and short set and he was wearing two pairs
4   of your shoes!
5 ROBIN: What?! Are you crazy?
6 PAT: And not only that, but he'd — he had your Dream Red
7   lipstick smeared all over his mouth! *(Yelping, ROBIN's*
8   *hand shoots up to her Dream Red lipstick covered lips.)*
9 PAT: So, do you think we oughta take him to the pound
10   now?
11 ROBIN: Grab the car keys! That sucker is — My Dream
12   Red?! Oh! Oh! I think I'm gonna puke!

Togetherness

Introduction

Nothing like togetherness! TINA and RINA are side by side, holding hands, and facing the audience. They suddenly exhale and relax. Not to give too much away, but they are the human personification of a *bra!*

1 TINA: What a relief! Is she ever going to lose any weight?
2 RINA: Well, if she doesn't, we're both going to be old before
3   our time.
4 TINA: Stretched out, worn out, and frayed. I already have
5   some of my stitches working loose.
6 RINA: I probably do, too, but I'm afraid to look. Has she
7   never head of spandex?
8 TINA: Oh, please, how about a sports bra?
9 RINA: *(Protesting)* I am not made for aerobics! I am delicate.
10   I am intricate. I cost twenty-one ninety-five at Victoria's
11   Secret for crying out loud!
12 TINA: I remember how pretty we were sitting on the shelf in
13   the store. We were displayed so nicely. Our own special
14   lighting. Our own special packaging. That picture of Elle
15   McPherson proudly wearing us.
16 RINA: Oh, to belong to Elle McPherson. Now there's
17   somebody who'd appreciate us.
18 TINA: But she *did* appreciate us.
19 RINA: Yeah, when?
20 TINA: When she first got us. We were a Valentine gift. What
21   was not to like?
22 RINA: I think it was the divorce that did it. That made us
23   just another pair to put on.
24 TINA: Yeah, I think you're right. You notice, she doesn't
25   wear *anybody* much anymore. At least, not around the

1   house. Not since she's by herself.
2 RINA: Yeah, it must be hard being alone. I can't imagine
3   being without you.
4 TINA: Yeah, we got it good. We're always together.
5 RINA: And I'm glad we're not one of those front-latch
6   jobbers, either. We'll always be together. Side by side.
7 TINA: That's right. Where one of us goes, the other one
8   goes, too!

About the Author

Michael Moore is a theatre practitioner with over thirty years experience. He holds a BSEd from Abilene Christian University and an MFA in Playwriting from Texas Tech University. He has taught at both the high school and college level. He is a playwright, director, teacher, and actor. He presently resides near Memphis, TN, with his wife, Helen, and their dog, Probee.

Order Form

Meriwether Publishing Ltd.
PO Box 7710
Colorado Springs, CO 80933-7710
Phone: 800-937-5297 Fax: 719-594-9916
Website: www.meriwether.com

Please send me the following books:

_____ **100 Duet Scenes for Teens #BK-B328**   **$17.95**
by Michael Moore
One-minute duos for student actors

_____ **Acting Duets for Young Women**   **$17.95**
#BK-B317
by Laurie Allen
8- to 10-minute duo scenes for practice and competition

_____ **Improv Ideas #BK-B283**   **$23.95**
by Justine Jones and Mary Ann Kelley
A book of games and lists

_____ **Comedy Scenes for Student Actors**   **$17.95**
#BK-B308
by Laurie Allen
Short sketches for young performers

_____ **275 Acting Games: Connected #BK-B314**   **$19.95**
by Gavin Levy
A workbook of theatre games for developing acting skills

_____ **102 Monologues for Middle School Actors** **$17.95**
#BK-B327
by Rebecca Young
Including comedy and dramatic monologues

_____ **Sixty Comedy Duet Scenes for Teens**   **$17.95**
#BK-B302
by Laurie Allen
Real-life situations for laughter

These and other fine Meriwether Publishing books are available at
your local bookstore or direct from the publisher. Prices subject to
change without notice. Check our website or call for current prices.

Name: _____ email:_____

Organization name: _____

Address: _____

City: _____ State: _____

Zip: _____ Phone: _____

❑ **Check enclosed**

❑ **Visa / MasterCard / Discover / Am. Express #** _____

Signature: _____ *Expiration date:* _____ / _____ *CVV code:* _____
           (required for credit card orders)

Colorado residents: Please add 3% sales tax.
Shipping: Include $3.95 for the first book and 75¢ for each additional book ordered.

❑ *Please send me a copy of your complete catalog of books and plays.*